INDEPENDENT STUDY PROGRAM

Teacher's Guide

INDEPENDENT STUDY PROGRAM

Teacher's Guide

Susan K. Johnsen, Ph.D.
& Kathryn Lee Johnson, Ed.S.

PRUFROCK PRESS INC.
WACO, TEXAS

Copyright ©2007 Prufrock Press Inc.

Printed in the United States of America.

No part of this book may be reproduced, translated, stored in a retrieval system, or transmitted, in any form or by any means, electronic, mechanical, photocopying, microfilming, recording, or otherwise, without written permission from the publisher.

At the time of this book's publication, all facts and figures cited are the most current available; all telephone numbers, addresses, and Web site URLs are accurate and active; all publications, organizations, Web sites, and other resources exist as described in this book; and all have been verified. The authors and Prufrock Press make no warranty or guarantee concerning the information and materials given out by organizations or content found at Web sites, and we are not responsible for any changes that occur after this book's publication. If you find an error or believe that a resource listed here is not as described, please contact Prufrock Press.

ISBN-13: 978-1-59363-231-1

Prufrock Press Inc.
P.O. Box 8813
Waco, TX 76714
(800) 998-2208
FAX (800) 240-0333
http://www.prufrock.com

Contents

Overview of the Independent Study Program 1

Chapter 1
Introducing the Independent Study Process................................25

Chapter 2
Selecting a Topic...37

Chapter 3
Organizing a Topic 49

Chapter 4
Asking Questions...67

Chapter 5
Using a Study Method 83

Chapter 6
Collecting Information..99

Chapter 7
Developing a Product 111

Chapter 8
Presenting Information..125

Chapter 9
Evaluating the Independent Study...139

Appendix A: Teacher Resources............................... 147
Appendix B: Student Resources 157
Appendix C: Assessment Forms 161
Appendix D: Resource Cards and Student Booklet Thumbnails .. 169
Glossary 205
References.. 209
About the Authors 211

Overview of the Independent Study Program

What is honored in a country will be cultivated there.
—Plato

What Is Independent Study?

We define independent study as a *process* that students use when they research a new topic by themselves or with others. This process is cyclical and includes a variety of steps that engage the students in acting like professionals, such as posing questions, gathering information related to the questions, organizing the information, and presenting the information to an audience. Along with the process, content focuses on "real-world investigations" (Renzulli & Reis, 1991, p. 131) and provides opportunities for students "to go beyond the usual time and space restrictions of most school activities" (Betts, 1985, p. 55). Kitano and Kirby (1986) add the important elements of teacher involvement: "Students conduct self-directed research projects that are carefully planned with the teacher and are monitored frequently" (p. 114). Therefore, independent study is

> a planned research process that (a) is self-directed; (b) is similar to one used by a practicing professional or authentic to the discipline; (c) is facilitated and monitored by the teacher; and (d) focuses on life-like problems that go beyond the regular class setting. (Johnsen & Goree, 2005, pp. 5–6)

Rationale

Independent study is the most frequently recommended instructional strategy for teachers of gifted and talented students (Clark, 2002; Colangelo & Davis,

2003; Coleman & Cross, 2005; Davis & Rimm, 1998; Rogers, 2002). Using this strategy, students are able to pursue a topic in greater depth at their own pace with professionals and others who are interested in the same area of study. The teacher can also use this method to provide for a wide range of individual differences by allowing students to select topics of interest and varying the complexity of the questions that direct the study. Most students, particularly those who are gifted and talented, enjoy instructional strategies that are meaningful and emphasize independence (Dunn & Griggs, 1985; Renzulli, 1977; Stewart, 1981). Their greatest interest in learning is to "learn something new and different" (Rogers, 2002, p. 277). However, whereas most students enjoy learning independently, they do not always have the necessary skills to complete a project successfully, so they need to learn the independent study process. Once they have acquired the critical independent study strategies, gifted students are able to become lifelong learners, capable of responsible involvement and leadership in a changing world (Betts, 1985).

10 Reasons to Use the Independent Study Program

1. Teaches an independent process for creating new knowledge.
2. Provides opportunities for authentic investigations of real-world problems that are beyond the traditional classroom curriculum.
3. Promotes deeper and more complex thinking.
4. Advances knowledge in selected areas of interest.
5. Supports self-paced learning.
6. Increases opportunities for working with practicing professionals who share the students' interest.
7. Stimulates the development of professional products.
8. Encourages students' self-reflections and self-evaluations.
9. Differentiates instruction based on individual interests, learning preferences, and content complexity.
10. Leads to lifelong learning and responsible involvement.

What Does the Independent Study Process Look Like?

We have identified nine different steps in the independent study process (see Figure 1). You will notice that these steps are not necessarily sequential, but are

Overview of the Independent Study Program

more cyclical and based on the students' progress. For example, in the fourth step, the students are supposed to ask questions. If the students don't have enough background knowledge, then they need to collect information about the topic (Step 6) before asking questions that are more meaningful. Similarly, the students may be collecting information (Step 6) and identifying more interesting questions that they would like to add to the study (Step 4). Therefore, each of these steps may lead to the next step, to previous steps, or to future steps based on the students' performance. In addition, you may decide to skip steps, guide the students through some of the steps, or allow the students to do some of the steps independently. For example, with young kindergarten students, you may choose to teach a specific study method such as collecting unbiased information, but with students who have more experience with independent study, you may want to allow them to select their own study methods that match their questions. For these reasons, the independent study process should be used as a framework, with you and the students developing each step more fully based on that particular student's prior knowledge and skills.

Program Components and Materials

Teacher's Guide

This Teacher's Guide provides:
- *Scope*: Lists in detail what the students are learning.
- *Chapters containing a series of lessons*: Teaches students the process of independent research. Included are step-by-step strategies related to the eight steps of basic research: selecting a topic, organizing a topic, asking questions, using a study method, collecting information, developing a product, presenting information, and evaluating the study. Each chapter with lessons is organized into the following components:
  - *About . . .*—Presents a brief overview and explanation of each lesson.
  - *Objectives*—Gives clear learning outcomes.

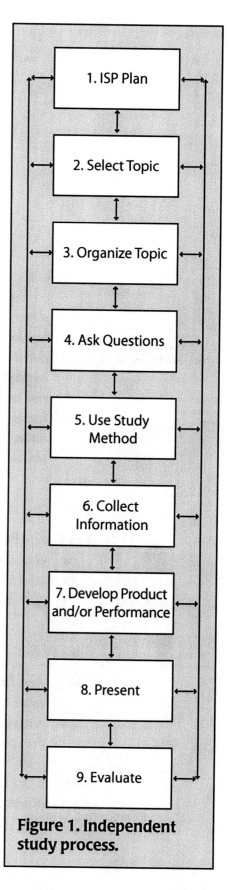

Figure 1. Independent study process.

- *Key Concepts*—Defines and explains a few of the main concepts that are important in each step of the independent study process.
- *Materials*—Lists items needed for teaching each step.
- *How Do I Teach . . .*—Provides guidelines for teaching each stage, including ways to model strategies to students and examples of students' work.
- *Ideas for Primary Students*—Suggests various ways to adapt the *Independent Study Program* for younger students.
- *Tips for Teachers*—Offers suggestions based on feedback from teachers who have used this program in their classrooms.
- *Evaluation Questions*—Asks pertinent questions about students' learning.

- *Appendices*: Provides four appendices. Appendix A contains teacher resources, including a scope of the independent study skills, class growth chart, conference planning guide, interest inventory, and parent letter. Appendix B contains student resources, including a handout on SCAMPER and note-taking and letter examples. Appendix C contains assessment forms, including a rubric, checklist, rating scales, and direct observation forms. Appendix D contains thumbnail pictures of the Resource Cards and Student Booklet pages.

Resource Cards

The Resource Cards offer:
- ideas for both students and teachers,
- information and examples for each step of the research process, and
- opportunities for students to learn the process independently.

Student Booklets

The Student Booklets are:
- consumable, write-in workbooks that relate to the Teacher's Guide, and
- instructional guides to help students plan and organize their own independent research projects.

They are most effectively used with whole-class and small-group instruction to support student learning—not simply given as a stand-alone workbook.

20 Strategies Used When Teaching Independent Study

A variety of strategies may be used when teaching independent study. Twenty of these are mentioned here and are used in the lessons throughout the book. For each strategy, we have provided a definition and when and how to use it. In all cases, remember to let the students be your guide when selecting strategies.

1. *Brainstorming* (generating new ideas; see Chapter 2, Lesson 1a; Chapter 3, Lesson 2)

Brainstorming is a process to help us think of many, varied ideas related to a topic. This technique is used by scientists, advertisers, writers, artists, and businesspersons to stimulate creative thinking. To brainstorm ideas, an individual student or a group gives as many varied ideas as possible related to some topic or problem. Ideas are recorded with no judgment. When brainstorming ends, an evaluation may then take place based on a purpose or a set of criteria.

For example, students might brainstorm areas of interest for an independent study, questions, products, or criteria for evaluation.

2. *Categorizing* (organizing knowledge; see Chapter 3, Lessons 1 and 5; Chapter 4, Lesson 4)

Categorizing is a process that is used to place ideas that have similar characteristics under a common heading. To categorize, you and/or the students can create headings and then place examples under the headings (a deductive process), or you and/or the students can identify examples and then create the headings based on the set of examples (an inductive process).

For example, the students might talk about dogs having fur, four legs, tails, and so on. They would then look at these examples and describe a heading that might be used to describe all of the examples (e.g., "appearance" or "how dogs look").

3. *Comparing and Contrasting* (clarifying the characteristics of concepts, process, or product; see Chapter 3, Lessons 3 and 5)

Comparing involves finding similar characteristics across examples, whereas contrasting involves finding different characteristics across examples. To compare or contrast, examples are presented and reviewed. The students examine how these examples are similar or different by describing "surface" features (how they look) and "structural" features (how they are used—underlying rules or broader categories).

For example, you may place examples of *facts* and *opinions* side by side or within Venn diagrams. You could then ask, "How are they alike?" and then, "How are they different?" The students would respond with characteristics of facts and characteristics of opinions.

4. *Conferencing* (monitoring student progress; any lesson)

A conference is a meeting between you and the student or a small group of students to monitor progress. Ideally, conferences are held on a daily basis, but should be held no less than once a week. During the conference, you will guide, listen to, encourage, and make suggestions for the students.

For example, you and the student(s) might talk about completed work, engage in a discussion about the topic, and confer about various independent study steps such as developing questions, collecting information on a topic, developing a product, or preparing for the presentation.

5. *Connecting to Previous Learning* (introducing a new content, process, or product; any lesson)

Connecting to previous learning involves identifying what the students already know and finding ways to build on the knowledge so that they achieve a more mature understanding. To connect to previous learning, you will ask questions about what the students know or observe how they respond to tasks. Based on what the students say or do, you will connect this previous knowledge to the new knowledge that is being taught.

For example, students may give examples from their lives about a particular concept such as *change* (e.g., baby to adult, moving from one house to another or from one school to another). If you are discussing the different forms of water, you could show how changes in water forms also change how something looks.

6. *Defining* (identifying the important characteristics of a content, process, or product; see Chapter 1, Lesson 1)

Defining is a process that is used to identify essential characteristics of a concept, a process, or a product for the purpose of creating a definition. To define, you or the students should provide examples of a particular concept, process, or product. The students then compare the examples and identify the important characteristics found in each. From these characteristics, a definition is created. To verify the definition, the students should check to see if their examples fit the definition.

For example, students may provide examples of *organizing*, and these are used to create a common definition of the term. The definition is then evaluated using the examples provided by the students by asking questions such as, "Would the definition describe Jeff's example?"

> 7. *Direct Instruction* (developing the characteristics of a concept, process, or product using examples and nonexamples; see Chapter 1, Lesson 2)

In direct instruction, you identify what is to be learned and systematically sequence examples and nonexamples of the concept, process, or product being learned. You then ask the students to apply the new knowledge in varied settings, as well as independently, to ensure that learning has occurred. During direct instruction, you tell the students about what they are learning and provide examples of the concept, process, or product. The students will then tell you about common characteristics across the examples. Once the students are able to describe the common characteristics and identify more positive examples, then you can show some nonexamples and have them discuss why the nonexample is not an example of the concept, process, or product. When discussing examples and nonexamples, you should compare examples and turn a nonexample into an example whenever possible.

For instance, the students will be learning how to identify a "good" study question. You first will have students compare examples of good study questions and identify important characteristics, such as "it requires more than one answer," "it might have different answers from different people," "it needs time to be studied," "it has information available for the study," and "it is useful or beneficial." Next, you will contrast examples of poor study questions with good study questions, such as "What are different types of clouds?" (poor) vs. "What are opinions regarding weather changes and global warming?" (good). You will then ask the students to change some of the poor study question examples into good study questions. Finally, you will ask the students to generate their own example of a good study question, using the presented characteristics as criteria.

> 8. *Establishing Criteria for Evaluation* (making decisions about the quality or value of a topic, question, or product; see Chapter 2, Lesson 2; Chapter 7, Lesson 2)

To establish criteria for evaluation, you or the students should generate ideas about the purposes they might use for selecting a theme, topic, question, product, and so on. These ideas are then organized into a set of comparison statements that are posed in the same direction (e.g., positive or negative). Each idea is then "tested" using each comparison statement or criterion. The comparison statements or criteria then may be revised based on the outcome or the effect on the selection.

For example, the students may identify several topics that they may want to study (e.g., Emperor Penguins, video games, space travel). The students would then generate ideas about the purpose for studying these topics such as interest, future career, friends like it, future issue for society, and so on. These purposes are then formed into comparison statements such as "most interesting to me," "most related to my future career," "most important issue for friends," and "most relevant to society."

9. *Using Metaphors or Analogies* (connecting to a picture, symbol, or word that is related to an entirely different concept set, to help clarify the characteristics of what is being taught; see Chapter 2, Lesson 1a; Chapter 5, Lesson 1)

Finding a metaphor or an analogy helps students connect what they know to what they don't know. To use a metaphor or an analogy, you can identify a concrete object, a picture or symbol, or a word that is connected to something that is being taught. The metaphor or analogy will share some of the characteristics of the new concept, process, or product. You then describe or demonstrate to students how the metaphor or analogy is similar to what is being learned.

For example, when teaching how to brainstorm, you might write the word *rainstorm* on the board, open an umbrella, and ask, "What happens in a rainstorm?" After the students respond, you can add a "B" in front of rainstorm and read aloud, *brainstorm*. You should elaborate that a brainstorm is similar to a rainstorm in many ways, but instead of raining drops of water, it rains thoughts and ideas. You then can help the students make further connections to the analogy by using the responses that the students made to the initial question (e.g., comparing lightning and lots of raindrops to sudden ideas that flash in your mind and many ideas).

10. *Modeling* (teaching something new—specifically a multistep process or technique for designing a product; see Chapter 6, Lesson 1; Chapter 7, Lesson 3)

Demonstrate for the students how to develop a product or how to do a specific process such as comparing, contrasting, brainstorming, and so on. To model, you should name the process or product and *show*, rather than tell, the steps in that process or in developing the product by writing them on the board or having a student checklist. You can then ask the students to watch as you follow the steps. You should discuss the process to check for understanding and then ask the students to demonstrate the process or the techniques in designing the product.

Overview of the Independent Study Program

For example, to model how to present an effective introduction to an oral report, you might begin in this way: Play the sound of a wolf howling—something that can be found in a public library or online. Tell the students,

> That was the sound of a wolf in the wild. Most of us have never heard that sound in real life, but what picture does it create in your mind? When you think of wolves, do you think of scary stories you've read about the Big Bad Wolf and werewolves or do you think of beautiful dog-like animals that look like German Shepherds? (Hold up two pictures, one that is a scary storybook wolf and one that is a beautiful dog-like photograph.) Today, I'm going to share with you some information I learned about wolves.

After you have shared your information, discuss what was effective about the way you presented your introduction (grabbed their attention, made a personal connection, showed pictures, and so on). Then, have the students list their ideas about making an effective oral report. Finally, share the steps for presenting an oral report (see Resource Card 106).

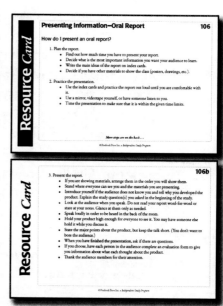

11. *Using Creative Problem Solving* (students have an ill-defined problem and need to decide what the problem is and how to solve it; see Chapter 3, Lesson 5)

Creative Problem Solving (CPS) is a process that includes these seven steps:
1. examining a "mess" or ill-defined problem,
2. identifying underlying problems,
3. stating the main problem,
4. identifying possible solutions,
5. selecting the best solution,
6. developing an action plan, and
7. implementing the plan.

To use CPS, you present the mess to the students and assist them in following some or all of the seven steps.

For example, you might create the following mess to share with the class:

Pablo asked the following questions: What are the characteristics of green herons? How do they develop? How might we attract more green herons to our local lake? Pablo has completed gathering information about his questions from the Web, from books, from an interview with a specialist, and from observing green herons at a nearby lake. He is now ready to organize his information and develop a product to share with the rest of the students in the fifth grade.

You would then ask the students to brainstorm some related problems, such as how to organize the information, identify information that is most related to the questions, and select a product that will be appropriate for the audience, and the like. After the students brainstorm all of the related problems, you can help them with the main problem statement by using this formula: In what ways or how might Pablo (who) organize the information (action) to address the questions (criterion) and develop a product (action) that is appropriate for the audience (criterion)?

Once the main problem is stated, the students can brainstorm some possible solutions and select the best solution by evaluating how well it meets the criteria—how well it addresses the questions and is appropriate for the audience in the example above. Finally, you can assist the students in identifying steps to implement the plan (i.e., organize the information, develop the product, and present it to the audience).

12. *Notice Special Features* (identifying the important characteristics of products; see Chapter 9, Lesson 1)

Noticing special features requires students to pay attention to the important characteristics of professional products. You can then have students use these features to develop their own products for their independent studies. Students may not use all of the features of professional products, but they will begin to notice and make decisions about what may make their product interesting and how they might use it to present information in a clear and understandable way.

For example, if students are going to write a nonfiction book about bears, they might look at several examples of how nonfiction writers present information in published texts. They might note special features of nonfiction books they like and then incorporate a few into their own book. Most nonfiction books contain:
- a table of contents,
- lessons,
- an index,

Overview of the Independent Study Program

- a glossary,
- pictures or illustrations that look real,
- an informative title,
- amazing facts,
- factual (real) information, and
- headings for different categories.

Younger students often like to emulate the *Magic School Bus* series because they notice the layers of information found in these books—facts listed on note cards in margins, vocabulary words on a chalkboard picture, fictional story in cartoon form with outlandish events related to the topic, dialogue in talk bubbles, humor with jokes and plays on words, and nonfiction information embedded throughout the text and detailed illustrations. They are able to notice the special features of the series, and then create their own characters and storyline for a piece of factual fiction.

13. *Paired Learning* (creating more opportunities for students to share information or respond to another's ideas; see Chapter 3, Lesson 1)

If you believe that two heads are better than one, then paired learning is a great strategy for you and your students. By working together in pairs, the students each have an opportunity to express their ideas about new information learned with a partner. The listener has the opportunity to hear something new, to think about it, and ask questions. The students can then switch roles. Try to structure the time together to maximize the benefits, such as having a class chart explaining what they are to do, modeling how to be a good teller and responder, and guiding students to use the time together effectively (see Figure 2).

14. *Questioning* (helping students think about a topic, theme, problem, or issue; any lesson)

Throughout the independent study experience, you will ask questions of your students to help them think, plan, organize, study, and present their findings. In questioning, you might want to use a question framework such as Bloom's Revised taxonomy or Paul's (1997) critical thinking strategies to help anticipate questions that might be asked when guiding a student through a particular independent study step or when leading a discussion. Throughout the independent study process, you will want to find ways to *ask*, rather than tell, students what to do.

For example, you might want to use some of the questions from Paul's (1997) framework to guide the students in selecting unbiased information:

How Partners Work Together	
Teller	**Responder**
• Tell your partner what you need. • Share information you have learned. • Listen to comments offered. • Thank the partner for helping. • Think about what to do next.	• Ask what your partner needs help with. • Listen to what your partner shares. • Tell something specific you like. • Suggest an improvement or idea. • Thank your partner for sharing.

Figure 2. Example of how partners work together.

- Why do you think that is true?
- Do you have any evidence for that?
- How might you go about finding out whether that is true?
- What other information do you need to know?
- Is the evidence believable?
- Is there reason to doubt the evidence?
- Who is in a position to know if that is the case?
- What would convince the audience?

15. *Scaffolding* (challenging students by presenting a task that is slightly more difficult than the previous task; any lesson)

The original meaning of the word *scaffold* was a "temporary platform used to elevate and support workers and materials during the construction, repair, or cleaning of a structure or machine" (Encyclopedia Britannica Online, n.d.) Teachers have transferred this graphic concept to mean the support that teachers give students as they "build" new skills and strategies. To scaffold, you may model, direct teach, ask questions, use prompts or cues, or use any similar strategies to gradually move students toward independent learning.

For example, in using prompts to assist students in formulating questions, you will use Resource Card 11 (Organizing a Topic—Description) that has descriptive statements to generate questions about the students' topics. If a student is studying bees, ask the student what she wants to know about bees, showing her Resource Card 11. You would ask, "Do you want to know about the bee's different parts, the different

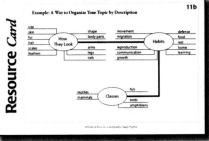

types of bees, the bee's contributions, . . . ?" The student indicates which of the areas is most interesting to her. You can show the student how to use a descriptive statement such as "its different parts" to formulate the question, "What are the bee's different parts?"

16. *SCAMPER* (generating more ideas; see Chapter 3, Lesson 5)

SCAMPER (Eberle, 1996; see Appendix B for a student handout) is a structured form of brainstorming to increase the number of ideas. Many inventions were developed using the SCAMPER techniques. SCAMPER is the acronym for:

- S   Substitute (Who or what else instead? Other ingredient, material, place?)
- C   Combine (Put several things together; blend.)
- A   Adapt or Add (What else is like it? How could it be changed?)
- M   Modify, Magnify, or Minimize (Change the meaning, add to it, or give it a new twist; make it bigger, longer, or taller; make it smaller, shorter, or narrower.)
- P   Put to other uses (Use in other places; use in a new way.)
- E   Eliminate (Take something away; make it smaller, lower, or shorter.)
- R   Rearrange or Reverse (Make another pattern or different sequence. What is the opposite? Can you turn it around?)

To teach students how to SCAMPER, write the acronym on the board and model the technique using a common object such as a pencil. You might say, "Someone thought to Combine a pencil and an eraser and put them together into one writing instrument. The pencil was Adapted to include an attached eraser. Someone Modified it and increased the diameter of pencils for young children." Once you have modeled all of the different techniques to generate new ideas about the pencil, you might give the students another object (e.g., notebook, cup, or shoe) to practice the technique, or you might see what other items students can think of that may have changed over time and identify which SCAMPER technique was used. (Think about how some modern tools came about, such as CDs, iPods, etc.)

For example, students might want to use the SCAMPER technique to generate ideas for a new game of checkers. They might decide to substitute new objects for play instead of using flat discs; combine checker rules with some of the chess rules; modify the board so that it is diagonal instead of square; eliminate some of the rules or add some new ones; and so on.

17. *Summarize* (synthesizing information that has been gathered; any lesson)

To summarize is to describe in one or two sentences the main ideas that have been presented or discussed. In summarizing, you or the students will take all of the statements that have been presented orally or in writing, identify the commonalities across the statements to create bigger ideas, and then write or say one or two sentences that incorporate the bigger ideas. To check the summary, the students may place the other sentences under the one or two sentences that were written to make sure that all of the ideas are represented. To assist with memory, students' comments during an oral discussion might be placed on a chart, and they could then summarize all of these comments into one or two sentences with major ideas.

For example, the students might identify one major idea from each of the sentences that they have written about inventions. They would then look at all of these ideas and put together the ones that appear to share some common characteristics. The shared ideas would then be combined into one or two summary sentences.

18. *Think-Aloud/Metacognitive Thinking* (clarify the process that was used in solving the problem; see Chapter 7, Lesson 3)

Think-aloud is a strategy that lets students hear the teacher's or other students' thought processes as they talk out loud about *how* they solved a problem. The students then use this reflection to solve similar problems. To use metacognitive thinking, you might ask a student who solved a problem effectively, "How did you go about solving that problem?" The student then describes aloud his or her problem-solving technique to you and/or other students. You and/or the student may want to enhance the oral presentation by adding a picture or web of the thinking process.

For example, you might think aloud in front of the class and model the process of asking higher level questions. You might say,

> Because I wanted to know more about Mozart, I decided first to ask some "W" questions, such as "What symphonies did Mozart compose?", "Who was Mozart's teacher?", "When did he begin composing?", "Where did he compose?", and so on. After I asked these questions, I wanted to create at least one or more higher level questions, so I thought, "In what new situation might I place either Mozart or his compositions?" I then asked, "What if Mozart had not lived in Austria but in England? What if Mozart had lived at an earlier or later time?" I decided that I would gather information on Mozart first and then decide which of those questions I would like to answer based on the information that I had gathered.

19. *Visualizing* (create a picture of the desired outcome; see Chapter 7, Lesson 3)

Visualization is a technique that astronauts have used for decades to imagine and picture in their minds how something might happen and how they would react. It is an underused strategy. Educators can implement visualization by having students create a vivid mental picture of a desired outcome. To visualize, you might ask the students to close their eyes and create a picture of their products in their minds. While the students' eyes are closed, you might say, "Think about its color . . . its shape . . . its size . . . how it will 'hook' the audience . . . how it will answer the questions about your topic?" Then have the students either orally describe or draw a picture of what they have visualized.

For example, you might ask the students to imagine how they might present their information to the class. You would ask them to see themselves arranging their materials prior to the presentation, standing where everyone can see them and the materials, introducing themselves, explaining the study questions, looking at the audience, speaking loudly in order to be heard in the back of the room, holding the product high enough for everyone to see it, stating the major points about the product, asking for questions at the end, and thanking the group for their attention. At the end of the visualization, students might want to practice their presentations either alone or in pairs.

20. *Webbing or Mapping* (using pictures or symbols to organize knowledge; see Chapter 3, Lesson 2)

When students web or map their ideas, a concept is placed within a circle and then linked to other concepts in other circles that are connected to the original circle. These concepts may be arranged hierarchically with major or superordinate concepts linked to lower order concepts, which are eventually linked to examples. To web or map, you might place the name of a concept in a circle and ask the students to think of an area that describes the concept, such as its features, its uses, attitudes about it, its underlying principles, and so on. Each of these areas is placed within a circle with branching circles that contain other concepts or examples.

For example, the students might link *dogs* to *appearance* (fur, four legs,), to *uses* (pets, work, hunting), and to *habits* (homes, reproduction, survival). (See Figure 3 for an example.)

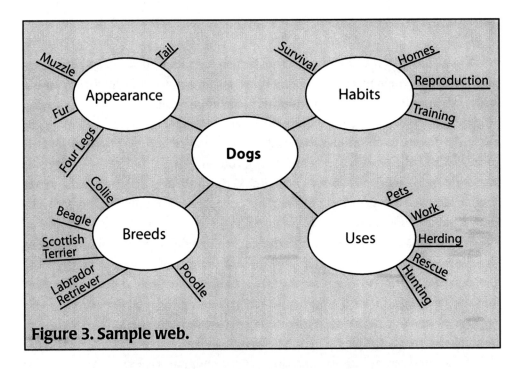

Figure 3. Sample web.

Scope of Independent Study Skills

The Independent Study Program provides a scope of all of the skills that are taught within the program, including the 14 different study methods (see Appendix A). Your school district might want to place this scope within a sequence and decide which skills should be taught at the primary, intermediate, middle school, and high school levels. The scope of skills might also be used to track student progress across grade levels. An example of an individual progress chart may be viewed in Appendix A.

Assessment

In almost every assignment, teachers assess student performance. The trend in recent years has moved away from traditional paper-and-pencil tests and more toward performance-based assessments that directly correspond to the complexity of what students are learning (e.g., science projects, lab reports, oral presentations, debates, interviews; Atkin, Black, & Coffey, 2001). Performance-based assessments provide the teacher and the students with not only more information about the important characteristics of the learning and performance goals, but also how near the students are to attaining these goals. In this way, the assessments may be used to help the student with strategies and skills needed to reach the goal (formative assessment) and in evaluating the quality of the final performance (summative assessment). The more clearly students understand the goals, the better able they will be to assess their own progress and improve their performance (Darling-Hammond, Ancess, & Falk, 1995).

With independent studies, students may be learning about various topics, using different methods, and creating a variety of products and/or performances. You will want to use assessments that provide information about the content, the processes, and the products or performances that are a crucial part of the students' learning. You will want to meet with the students frequently to determine how close they are to attaining the skills needed to reach their goals.

Assessment tools included in the *Independent Study Program* use a variety of methods for judging the quality of the content, the processes, and the products and/or performances (see Appendix C). You may decide which assessments are most appropriate for individual students or your class. Examples can be used as they are or adapted as needed. Some assessments will be for the teacher and others will be self-reflections by the students.

Assessments found in Appendix C include:
- *a rubric*—a set of characteristics that guide how students will be assessed;
- *a checklist*—a list of items or points for consideration about how to complete a project;
- *rating scales*—an assessment of particular characteristics on a scale according to how much or how little quality it shows. Sometimes the scale is numerical, such as 1–5, and sometimes the scale lists qualitative phrases; and
- *direct observations*—a way of recording what teachers notice about a student's learning.

Managing Independent Studies in the Classroom

Before you begin managing independent studies, you will want to consider how to arrange the classroom, organize materials, schedule time, and keep records. The way you choose to manage your classroom will depend on your resources and available space. Listed below are suggestions based on the most effective ways we've seen classrooms organized.

Classroom Arrangement

- Set up a table or corner of the classroom and designate it as a research center. Computers, books, magazines, and other resource materials might be

placed there. Pictures and questions about a specific class topic or individual topics might be posted on a bulletin board as a focus.
- If students are studying several different topics, student-made bulletin boards or tri-fold display boards might showcase all of their questions with pictures, photographs, and key words.
- Have a place in the classroom, such as a portion of the chalkboard, a dry erase board, or a laminated teacher schedule poster, where the student can sign up for extra help as needed. After whole-class instruction, the teacher might have time for individual or small-group meetings for students who need assistance with individual studies.

Organization of Materials

- Provide students with or have them supply three-ring binders to store all of their information.
- Help students to set up individual file folders on the computer to hold their files of collected information.
- Have a box or central place to keep all Student Booklets, such as a designated table or desk. It helps keep students organized to have everything located in one place for easy accessibility.
- Laminate the Resource Cards to make them more durable. Store them in a small box, so that students can thumb through them quickly. Another idea is to punch holes in the corners and keep the cards on a metal ring.
- Bookmark some Web sites for research topics that will be particularly helpful to your students. Let students set up individual files on the computer to house their Internet findings, take and store notes in Word documents, and include photographs and graphics.

Scheduling

- Make the independent study part of the class schedule, with time set aside each day for research. Students tend to lose focus if they have only one day each week to pursue their studies.
- Plan an entire unit that focuses on teaching the class how to conduct independent studies. Increasing student expertise will assist them in completing more studies independently.
- Plan time to teach each independent study skill, either individually, with a small group, or with the entire class.

Overview of the Independent Study Program

- When students are working independently on their studies, meet with them at least once a week individually to check on their progress. This schedule of individual teacher conferences might be kept on the chalkboard, in the student's folder, or on a bulletin board.
- Use pretests in the core subjects in the classroom to provide more research time for students who already have learned the concepts that the rest of the class is studying. Curriculum compacting forms suggested by Winebrenner (2001) are good resources to have.

Record Keeping

Keep a class chart to track each student's progress through the independent study process (see Figure 4).

When doing class studies, some teachers keep track of what students are doing using the theme that is being studied. For example, one teacher created a bulletin board depicting the solar system, which was the theme of the class study. Each student then created a rocket that moved from the topic planet, to the collecting information planet, and so on. Some tips for record keeping are listed below.

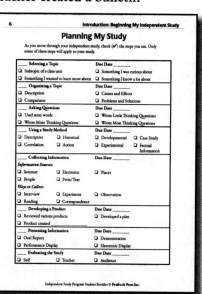

- Have each student keep a record in a folder or on the computer that describes what tasks have been completed each day.
- Use the Student Booklet as a record-keeping system for each student (see p. 6 in the Student Booklet). On the back of the plan, the students might reflect on their progress each day, citing areas of strengths and weaknesses.
- Use the Scope of Independent Study Skills (see Appendix A) and identify specific skills that you want the students to learn during this study. List these on a record-keeping form, along with possible resources. The students would then use this form to list resources that they are using to learn a specific skill. During the teacher conference, the students can share completed work and determine their progress on learning particular skills (see Figure 5).
- A modified record-keeping form that includes more specific skills might be used for a group or individual within the classroom. In this example, the student and teacher focus on developing one product (see Figure 6).

Selecting a Topic	Organizing a Topic	Asking Questions	Using a Study Method	Collecting Information	Developing a Product	Presenting a Product	Evaluating a Product
Elle Cliff Rasheed	Olivia	Taylor	Maria	Alicia Alex Jacob	Sarah Oshna		

Figure 4. Class chart of progress through independent study steps.

Skill	Resources Used (Expert Interviews, Surveys, Books, Journals, Media, Newspapers, Historical Documents, Internet, Other)	Conference
Topic Selection: Evaluate topic		
Organization: Use problems and solutions		
Questions: Use Most Thinking to examine problems		
Method: Examine improvement (Action Research)		
Method: Reliability of instrument		
Collect Information: Summarize notes		
Product		
Presentation		
Self-Evaluation of Action Research		
Self-Evaluation of Product		

Figure 5. Individual skill record form example.

Overview of the Independent Study Program

Name	Skill 1 Evaluate Topic	Skill 2 Most Thinking Questions	Skill 3 Survey	Skill 4 PowerPoint Presentation	Skill 5 Self-Evaluation	Conference
Ashley						
James						
Krystal						
Marlo						
Paige						
Roberto						
Schyler						
Samuel						
Thomas						
Zach						

Figure 6. Group skill record form.

Chapter 1 Overview

What is independent study?

- A self-directed process students use when researching a topic by themselves or with others.

What resources do students and teachers have?

- *Student Booklet*—A workbook that organizes and guides students through the independent study process.
- *Resource Cards*—A set of cards that presents additional information and examples about each step of the independent study.

Chapter 1
Introducing the Independent Study Process

There is danger in probing the future with too short a stick. Excellence takes time.
—E. Dale

About Introducing the Independent Study Process

To introduce independent studies, we asked a class of students, "What is an independent study?" James raised his hand and answered, "It's a research paper." We were somewhat surprised that an elementary student would have such a narrow concept of the independent study process. Since that time, we have learned that it is not unusual to find that when students hear the words *independent study*, they automatically think of note cards, written materials, and written reports about a teacher-selected topic—not always a pleasant experience from the student's perspective.

The independent study process described in this manual broadens these students' conceptions and presents students with options for the topics they will study, how they will study these topics, and what products or performances they will share with the audience.

In this lesson, we will provide an overview of the independent study process and how to develop a plan with each of the students. You will learn how to introduce independent studies and how to use the Resource Cards and the Student Booklets. This beginning step is important for providing an overview, sharing interests in new topics, encouraging students to think deeply, and providing a framework that guides their research.

Objectives

1. The students will define independent study.
2. The students will describe the steps involved in an independent study project.

3. The students will develop a plan that includes a timeline for each step in the independent study process.

Key Concepts

- *Independent study*—A process that you apply when you research a new topic by yourself or with others.
- *Research steps*—The steps you follow when you complete an independent study.

Materials for Teaching

- Resource Cards
- Student Booklets (pp. 1–8)
- Examples of some independent study projects completed by students in previous years, if possible.

Evaluation Questions

1. Did the students define independent study?
2. Given an independent study plan, did the students describe each step? Did primary students arrange the icons in order (see Ideas for Primary Students, p. 33)?

Introducing the Independent Study Process

Lesson 1: Defining Independent Study

1. Write on the board the words *independent study*. Ask your students to give examples of what they think these words mean and write their responses on the board (e.g., doing something by yourself, looking up information in books and on the Internet, projects).

2. Have the students compare the examples and identify what important characteristics the examples have in common. Use these characteristics to write a class definition of this term.

3. Write the *Independent Study Program's* definition of independent study on the board: "Independent study is the self-directed process you use when you research a new topic by yourself or with others."

4. Compare the students' definition with the one that you have written. Have them describe the similarities and differences. The discussion might address what is meant by *self-directed, process, research*, and *new topic*.

5. Ask the students to summarize the discussion or you can summarize the discussion by saying, "Independent study is a way to think deeply about something that's important to us, ask questions about it, and then try to answer those questions." You might vary this explanation based on the age and level of your students.

6. If the students are going to share their final products with a particular audience, tell them the type of group that will use their products or hear their information. Students will be more motivated to do a study if it is interesting to them, and if they know that it will be useful and interesting to others.

Lesson 2: Introducing the Independent Study Steps

1. Explain to the students that they will be learning the steps needed to do an independent study. Distribute the Student Booklets and have them write their names on the front. Tell them that this booklet will help guide them through their study and is a place where they can keep their ideas and notes.

2. Have students open their Student Booklets to Chapter 1: Introduction: Beginning My Independent Study (see p. 5). To review, have them write down their definition of independent study and what the study will mean to them.

3. Now, have them turn to Planning My Study in their Student Booklets (see p. 6). Explain, "These steps will help you dig more deeply into a subject and guide you through the research process." If possible, have several products that were created by students in previous years. If you don't have any available, you might want to come up with several products to model the range from poor to quality studies. Using these products, briefly explain to students each step in the process (or the ones that they will be using during their study if you choose to limit them) listed below:

    - *Selecting a Topic*—Students will choose a topic to study that you are interested in learning more about. Show the products and say, "What were these students' topics? How might you know if they were interested in them?"

    - *Organizing a Topic*—In this step, students will identify what part of their topic is most interesting to them and narrow the topic so that it is easier to ask questions. Show the products and have the students notice that each product has a broader

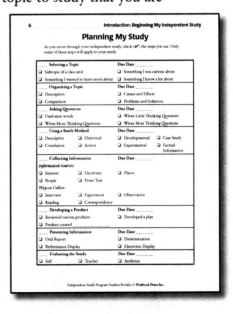

Introducing the Independent Study Process

topic such as *dogs*, but that the research focused on only one part of the topic (e.g., how to train dogs).

- *Asking Questions*—Every good research project begins with a question—something that students want to know and find out more about. Students will look at how to ask deep, meaningful questions using the "W" and "H" words—who, what, when, where, why, and how. Using the example products, share the students' questions. Write these questions on the board so that the students can examine them throughout the discussion of the remaining steps. Ask, "Did the students' products relate to their questions?" Emphasize how the questions are the driving force behind the entire independent study and ultimately determine the type of product or performance that they will create.

- *Using a Study Method*—There are many ways of studying students' questions. This step will help the students match their questions to the best study method. Using the sample products, share how each of the students studied his or her questions. For example, the student who wanted to know how to train dogs decided to use an action research study—examining an improvement to solve a problem. She first identified a "trick" that she wanted her dog to perform such as retrieving a stick. She then collected some information to show how many times the dog retrieved the stick, which at the beginning was zero—the dog just played with the stick. Next, she decided to use treats every time the dog brought the stick to her, recording the number of retrievals. At the end of her study, when the dog was retrieving the stick on a regular basis, she noted the most important influences that affected her dog's retrieval of sticks.

- *Collecting Information*—There are many sources and ways to gather knowledge to answer the students' questions (e.g., books, interviews, surveys, Internet, experiments, observations, e-mail, letters). Students will use the resources that best answer their questions. Using the sample products, tell how the students collected information. For example, you might describe how the student who collected information about how to train dogs interviewed dog trainers, read books, and visited Web sites.

- *Developing a Product*—Students will decide the best way to show what they've learned by creating something that answers their questions and is appropriate for the audience. Allow the students to examine the sample products again. At this time, have the students examine the questions related to the sample products and determine if the products and/or performances answered the questions. Hopefully, you will have some products that do and some that don't. For example, the student who studied how to train dogs might have created a video of a trainer working with a dog and/or a book of methods for training dogs. Let the students decide if the student's product(s) answered all of the questions.

- *Presenting Information*—Students will share their research findings with other people so that others can learn more about the topic. The students will decide the best way to present the information to others. Using the sample products, present the information to the students. Provide a positive example and a poor example of presenting the product. For example, you might stand in front of the product, talk too softly, make no eye contact with the students, talk too fast, and so on, which would model a poor presentation. Have the students indicate what you did correctly and what you did incorrectly for each presentation you make.

- *Evaluating the Study*—The best way to make something better is to think about what students did well and how they might improve next time. They will reflect about the process of independent study, as well as their product and presentation. Using the sample products, have the students discuss how they think that the products might be improved.

4. Have the students review the Planning My Study section in their Student Booklet on p. 6. If the students will be presenting their products to a particular audience, identify the date, and who the audience will be.

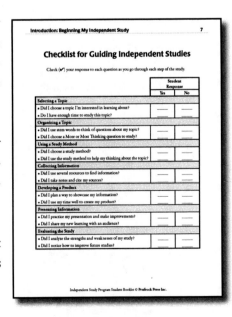

5. Fill in any other due dates that are currently known. These dates are very helpful for the students in managing their time throughout the independent study process.

6. Share the Checklist for Guiding Independent Studies (see p. 7 of Student Booklet). Tell students

that they will be able to use this page as a record of their progress. For example, when they select a topic, they will ask themselves the two questions found under that heading, "Did I choose a topic I'm interested in learning about? Do I have enough time to study this topic?" If they answer "yes" to each of these questions, then they are ready to move on to the next step. If they are not able to answer "yes," they may want to schedule a conference with the teacher.

7. Next, show students the Conference Planning Guide on p. 8 of the Student Booklet. Note that you may want to make several copies of this page so that students will have extra copies when they want to schedule a new conference. Say, "You will be able to use this conference planning guide in two ways—when you complete a step and are ready to move to the next step in the independent study process or when you need some assistance in completing a step. For example, you might be having trouble deciding on a particular topic and want to talk with me about your ideas. On the lines at the bottom of the page, you would write, 'I need some help in deciding about an independent study topic.'"

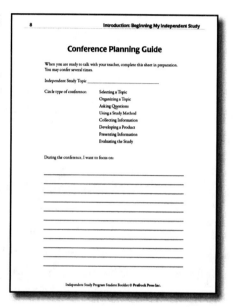

8. Conclude the lesson by having the students orally define independent study and describe the steps involved in an independent study project.

Lesson 3: Introducing Independent Study Resources

1. Hold up the Resource Cards to the students and inform them that these cards will give them information as they move through the steps of their independent studies. Share Resource Card 9: Selecting a Topic—Examples, and say, "You may be wondering what topic you might want to study. This card may help you. It has topics organized from A to Z." Read some of the topics to the students.

2. Pass out one card from the stack to each student and ask each one to describe the card's special features (e.g., the name of the step is at the top of the card, the card provides examples or steps, the card is color-coded according to the step, and so on). Ask how the Resource Cards might be helpful to them during their study (e.g., give examples so I can understand something better, present lots of ideas in case I'm stuck, tell me how to do something, etc.).

3. Give students some time to peruse the Resource Cards in small groups. They might talk afterwards as a class about some interesting information they found on the cards. Tell them where the cards will be kept and state your guidelines for using them.

Introducing the Independent Study Process

Ideas for Primary Students

- You may want to simplify the independent study definition by saying, "An independent study is a way of learning more about something that you are interested in."

- You might want to teach each of the steps using a corresponding icon: (a) for asking questions—a question mark; (b) for using a study method—a magnifying glass; (c) for collecting information—a suitcase; (d) for developing a product—scissors; (e) for presenting—an open mouth; and (f) for evaluating—a smiling face and a frowning face.

- Simplify the independent study process by eliminating choices within some of the steps, choosing methods that are developmentally appropriate, and modifying the complexity of the questions. For example, in formulating questions, you may focus the study on developing question stems (W's and H's) and not on developing more complex questions using Bloom's taxonomy. For the study method step, you might have students learn how to collect factual information (see Resource Cards 21–22) or conduct simple experiments. When gathering information, you might choose methods that do not require writing such as surveys or interviews. Similarly, in developing products, you might have the student demonstrate an experiment or develop a video instead of writing a report.

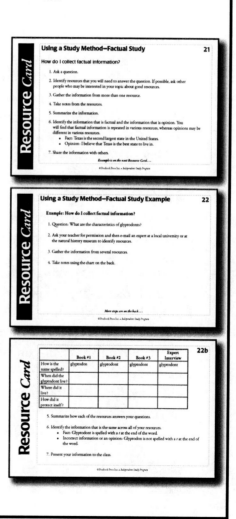

Tips for Teachers

- *Note to parents.* When you initiate the first independent studies with your class, you will want to send a note home to the student's parents, describing their role in their child's independent study (see an example of a parent letter in Appendix A).

- *Teach a method.* If you want the students to collect information using a specific method such as note taking, you will find it helpful to teach this method before beginning the study so that the flow of the independent study is not interrupted.

- *Limit choices.* When teaching a whole class to conduct independent studies for the first time, it is wise to limit choices for each of the steps to the number of groups or topics that you are able to manage successfully. For example, you might decide to limit studies to topics related to Ancient Egypt. The students could then choose topics from a range of possibilities (e.g., pyramids, mummies, culture, medicine, and so on), but you would have them rank order their top three choices. Using these choices, you would then place the students into three groups according to one of their top interests. You might also limit choices throughout the study, having students gather information from similar sources—books, Internet, and experts, for example—and having them all share their information with others through "museum exhibits." In this way, you will be able to work with the class as a whole to teach certain steps in the independent study process.

- *Use themes.* When working with the entire class, themes are helpful in providing a broader range of possible topics. For example, when a class studied the theme of *structures*, students chose to design a city and conducted research in a variety of areas: the structure of political systems (democracy), the structure of the environment (climate, flora, fauna, topography), the structure of the economy (monetary system), the structure of communication (media), the infrastructure (utilities, roads), and so on. For their end product, they constructed a prototype of a city, complete with a daily newspaper, an economy, stores, elections, and a new mayor.

- *Show checklist.* Show students how they will be evaluated *before* they begin their studies. You might use a checklist to help guide their thinking and organization.

How do students select their topics?

- *Individual interest*—Students may select individual topics to study that they are personally interested in learning more about.
- *Within a class theme*—A topic can be related to a broad theme or issue.

What are some ways to study a topic?

- *Single student*—Students work individually on a topic of interest.
- *Small group*—Several students may work together to study a common topic, but focus on different study questions.
- *Whole class*—All students study a common topic, but focus on various aspects of that topic through independent research.

Chapter 2 Overview

Chapter 2
Selecting a Topic

You are today where your thoughts have brought you.
You will be tomorrow where your thoughts take you.
—J. Allen

About Selecting a Topic

We remember the day we walked into a classroom and Ahmed asked us to take him to the library to look for books about birds. "Birds?" one of us asked. "I'm going to do a study of birds," he said. When he looked over the shelves and shelves of books about birds, his face fell and he slumped into a chair, mumbling, "I'll never be able to read all of these books." We asked him to tell us how he decided to study birds, and he told us the story of a whippoorwill that sang every evening in the woods behind his house. One fall night, he didn't hear the song and wondered what had happened. Then Ahmed's eyes lit up, and we could almost see that invisible light bulb over his head click on. "Hey," he jumped out of his seat. "I'll see if there are any books just on whippoorwills." He had found his topic—the *real* subject he wanted to study. And, it was small enough to study in depth.

The Selecting a Topic lessons guide students in identifying ideas for topics of interest or subtopics of a class unit. This is the point where you may need to set parameters to help your students begin a research project.

Objective

The students will select a specific topic to study from a variety of possibilities using evaluation and resources.

Key Concepts

- *Topic*—A subject or area that students may study.
- *Topic evaluation*—To compare reasons for selecting a particular topic to study.

Materials for Teaching

- Resource Cards 4, 8, and 9
- Student Booklets (pp. 9–14)

Evaluation Questions

1. Given several topics, did the students evaluate each one using relevant criteria?
2. Did the students select a topic that could be studied with available resources within the specified time frame?

Selecting a Topic 39

Lesson 1a: Identifying Topics for Independent Studies Based on Student Interest

1. Explain to the students that they will learn about selecting a topic for study. Ask the students if they have thought of some ideas that they might want to study. List these on the board. Describe how these ideas are called *topics*—names or phrases for large amounts of information.

2. Tell them that you are going to show them some ways of identifying even more topics that they might want to study before they make their final decision.

3. Write the word *rainstorm* on the board. Pop open an umbrella and ask, "What happens in a rainstorm?" (Students may say raindrops fall, thunder cracks, dark clouds gather, lightning flashes, wind blows, it floods, and so on.) Note that if you are working with one student, instead of using this brainstorming activity, you might want to use Resource Card 4 to gather more ideas.

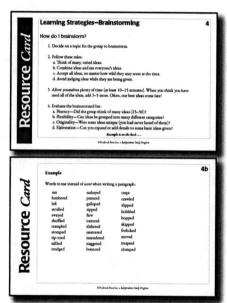

4. Now, put a "B" in front of *rainstorm* and read aloud the word *brainstorm*. Inform students that a brainstorm is similar to a rainstorm in many ways. But, instead of raining drops of water, it rains thoughts and ideas. Let them talk about what could happen in a brainstorm (e.g., ideas gather in our minds, a few thoughts come out, lots of thoughts join in when other people think of ideas, ideas pepper down, ideas fly through the air like wind). Help them make the analogy.

5. Summarize on the board the rules of brainstorming—ways to make brainstorming most effective.

   Brainstorming Rules
   - Think of many, varied ideas.
   - Combine and use everybody's ideas.
   - Accept all ideas, no matter how wild they may seem at the time.
   - Avoid judging ideas while they are being given.

6. Have the students brainstorm more topics. Write these on the board.

7. Write the following categories on a chart, dry-erase board, or chalkboard: A Problem I Want To Solve, A Fact I Want to Prove, Something I Want to Learn to Do, Something I Want to Know More About, and Other Topics. Ask the students to brainstorm ideas under each heading. Have the students work individually or in a small group to place their ideas together into different categories. Have the students share their categorized lists.

8. Now, have the students open their Student Booklets to p. 9 and answer the questions to determine more ways of identifying topics.

9. Using the lists they have made, the students will need some class time to think about which topic they want to study. Depending on their skill level, you most likely will need to guide them in finding information about possible topics. You can help by:
   - bringing books and magazines to the classroom in the areas of interest or have the students go to the library and browse in their general topic area;
   - having students bring resources from home that relate to their areas of interest;

Selecting a Topic

- identifying experts at colleges or in the community that might be able to share information and allowing the students to e-mail these experts for some information; and
- bookmarking Web sites that relate to students' topics.

Lesson 1b: Identifying Subtopics for Independent Studies Related to a Class Unit

1. If you will be conducting independent studies on a topic the whole class will be studying, you must first identify a unit that would lend itself for a variety of independent studies (e.g., the solar system, change).

2. Identify possible subtopics that might be of interest to the students. For the solar system, you might select black holes, the planets, stars, origins of the system, interplanetary space travel, and so on.

3. Introduce the possibility of studying subtopics by saying to the students, "You are going to be studying _____ (e.g., the solar system) during the next month. I would like for you to have an opportunity to study some topics related to _____ (e.g., the solar system) in greater depth and have made a beginning list of some of these subtopics." List these subtopics on the board.

4. Have the students look at Finding Subtopics in their Student Booklets on p. 11. Say, "Write the topic that we are studying together on the topic line. Now, list the subtopics that are interesting to you on the lines below. Add any new ones that you would like to study about _____ (e.g., the solar system)."

5. After the students have had some time to list these subtopics, have them share any new subtopics that they have listed. Allow other students to add these subtopics to their lists.

6. Now, ask each of the students to circle three of the subtopics that they would like to learn more about.

7. Take up the Student Booklets and review each student's choices. Group the students according to their interests.

8. Share the subtopics and the groupings with the class. Have each of the groups follow the steps of the independent study program.

Lesson 2: Evaluating the Topics

1. At the conclusion of their research, students may be ready to select a topic. However, sometimes it's hard to choose just one topic when there are several interesting possibilities. Using the chart on p. 12 in the Student Booklet, explain how to systematically evaluate several topics in order to select the most appropriate one for the student. Use the example of a completed chart to explain the process.

2. On the blank grid (see Student Booklet, p. 14), have students place several topics that they might want to study on the lines listed under *Topics*. (If the students are going to conduct a group study, have them vote on five topics to evaluate.)

3. To develop some evaluation criteria, ask the students to think of some reasons that they might want to study a particular topic. Some possible evaluation criteria include:
    - Which topic is the *most* interesting to me?
    - Which topic is the *most* useful?
    - Which topic will have the *most* information to study?
    - What information would be *easiest* to find?
    - Which topic do I know the *most* about?
    - Which topic can I study *best* with the time that I have?
    - Which topic can I study *best* with the resources that I have?

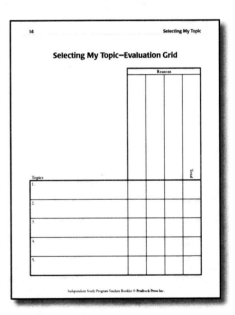

4. Have each student decide on three criteria and write them on the lines at the top of his or her chart.

Selecting a Topic

5. Have students look at one criterion at a time. They should ask themselves the question and put a "5" (or the number of topics being judged) in the box next to the topic that best fits the criterion. They should put a "1" next to the topic that fits the criterion the least. A "4" is placed by the next best, a "2" for the next least, and a "3" for the one that is left over. When they have judged each topic against each criterion, they will add the numbers next to each solution and put the sum in the Total box. The highest total becomes the best topic to study.

   Note: Sometimes this evaluation process helps the student identify a single topic. However, sometimes the student identifies a different topic than the one that is selected using the evaluation process. If so, still allow the student to select the topic that is the most interesting one to him or her.

6. Conclude this lesson by probing, "What have you learned about selecting a topic? Describe the process that you used in identifying a study topic. What resources and methods helped you the most? The least? What would you do the same or differently the next time?"

Ideas for Primary Students

- Asking students to share their collections and/or at-home activities will provide some clues to their interests. You might want to use an interest inventory (see Appendix A) to gather more information about the student. Using their interests might help them focus on a topic for their first independent study.

- Sometimes students will select a topic that is interesting to them but the resources are too technically advanced for them. They need more background knowledge before they will be able to study the topic. For example, Alan was interested in how pictures were conveyed via satellite. As we gathered resources, we found that they were quite technical and beyond his level of knowledge. With teacher guidance, he decided to study how sound was conveyed—a topic that lends itself to simple experimentation, which would build his knowledge and address his interest in telecommunications.

Tips for Teachers

- *Create topic bulletin board.* Because interest in topics develops over time, you might want to provide a topic bulletin board or topic box. In this way, when students have questions about topics that demand more time than available during a single class period, they can add these to the bulletin board or put them in the topic box for study at a later time.

- *List subtopics.* If you want students to study a subtopic of a unit you are teaching, generate a list of possible subtopics and have them rank order those that are most interesting to them. Form groups using their interests and have each group follow the rest of the steps for the independent study.

- *Discuss current issues.* Current issues provide many opportunities for topics. For example, adolescent students appear to be interested in issues related to global warming, evolution, downloading music, gender differences, and genetic manipulation. Use these topics as a springboard to a variety of independent study topics.

In what ways might topics be organized?

- *Description*—A written or verbal explanation of something, often organized by webbing or classifying.
- *Comparison*—Examining two or more things in order to discover similarities and differences between them.
- *Causes and effects*—Looking at the reasons why something happens and the changes that occur as a result of an action.
- *Problems and solutions*—Exploring a difficult situation, question, or puzzle that needs to be solved and possible ways to resolve the difficulty.

Chapter 3 Overview

Chapter 3
Organizing a Topic

If I have succeeded in my inquiries more than others, I owe it less to any superior strength of mind than to a habit of patient thinking.
—Sir Isaac Newton

About Organizing a Topic

Once students have topics, what do they do next? Do they brainstorm questions? Do they read about their topic, talk to experts, and then think of questions? Do they know how to think about their topic to allow them to ask relevant questions? This lesson addresses the last question. It helps students structure their thinking about a topic so that they will be able to formulate questions that relate to their interests.

This step was added after an experience with a third-grade classroom that wanted to study the topic of "space." We asked the class what they might want to learn and what questions they might want to ask. We used the "Ws" to prompt them. Immediately, hands were raised and these types of questions emerged: When will the aliens arrive on earth? Where do aliens live? What do they look like? It became quite clear that the students needed to gather more information so that their questions would be based on a foundation of knowledge, not popular media. At that point, we stopped asking questions and listed some of the descriptive areas that needed to be researched (e.g., parts of the solar system—stars, planets; travel in the solar system; life in the solar system). The class divided themselves into smaller interest groups and began their research. They needed knowledge before they were ready to ask logical questions.

Knowledge is built in layers with observations, facts, and basic concepts first, then generalizations and principles, and, finally, theories. If a student attempts to formulate a question without a basic understanding of the topic, the question may be superficial or even fanciful.

In this lesson, we will review four ways to organize topics that should be helpful to you and your students. Students will learn some ways of thinking about their topic that make sense. As needed, they will learn how to describe their topic, how to compare their topic with other topics, how to examine causes and effects that influence their topic, and how to solve problems.

Objective

1. The students will organize their topics using one or more methods, such as descriptions, comparisons, causes and effects, or problems and solutions.

Key Concepts

- *Organize*—To arrange information in a way that will help the student formulate questions.
- *Descriptions*—A written or verbal explanation of something, often organized by webbing or classifying.
- *Comparisons*—Examining two or more things in order to discover similarities and differences between them.
- *Causes and effects*—Looking at the reasons why something happens and the changes that occur as a result of an action.
- *Problems and solution*—Exploring a difficult situation, question, puzzle, or issue that needs to be solved and possible ways to resolve the difficulty.

Materials for Teaching

- Resource Cards 10–14
- Student Booklets (pp. 15–23)
- Several nonfiction books/picture books that show various ways to organize (Eyewitness Books are especially helpful.)
- Magazines and newspapers that identify problems and/or issues

Evaluation Questions

1. Given several ways to organize a topic, did the students select one that is relevant to their topics?
2. Did the students describe the process for organizing a topic using one of the four methods?

3. Were the students able to describe some gaps in their knowledge to formulate questions?

Lesson 1: Introducing the Students to Organizing a Topic

1. Write the word *organize* on the board. Ask students to describe how they organize things and ideas and write their examples in the Student Booklet on p. 15 (e.g., alphabetically, by color, having a file or box, computer folders, notebooks, and so on).

2. Have students share in pairs the different ways that they organize things or ideas. (See Paired Learning on p. 11.) They might want to think about collections that they have at home or ways that they organize their school materials. Have them compare their organization examples and identify one way that they are all alike. Have one of the group members share this similarity with the class, and write these ideas on the board or a chart. Ask, "How does organizing things or ideas help us?" Students might respond that they are able to find things easier, find what they have more of and what they are missing, put things together that are related, separate things that are different, think about things in a different way, and so on. Have them notice that organizing things is similar to how they might organize ideas. It helps them see how these are related to one another and what they may need to know to fill in any missing relationships or gaps.

3. Now, help students make some meaning of these ideas by providing the following definition for organizing a topic: "Organizing a topic means to arrange it in a way that will help you find specific questions to ask."

4. Next, tell students that they will later use one of the four ways to organize their topic that are listed on p. 15 in their Student Booklet, but that you will teach them one method today—*description*.

5. For most students, organizing their topics by description will be appropriate because students need to know the specific characteristics about their topic before they can compare it to other topics, examine influences, or solve

Organizing a Topic

problems. You might begin by teaching the whole class how to organize by description. If students already know how to organize a topic using descriptions, you will want to teach the students the other methods as needed. Each method is described in the lessons that follow.

Lesson 2: Organizing by Descriptions

1. Write the word *description* on the board. Tell the students, "When you describe something, you tell about it or explain in detail so that the reader or listener clearly understands. That is exactly what you do when you organize by description."

2. Put a sample topic in the middle of the board that they will all know something about, such as *dogs*. Circle it and web students' ideas about what they know about dogs (e.g., have fur, have four legs, bark, live in houses or outside, different sizes and colors).

3. Be amazed together about the number of different ideas that might be studied about a topic. Puzzle a moment about how you might explain this information to other people, because it is such a hodgepodge on the board. Elicit their ideas about how they might organize this large amount of information.

4. Guide students to notice, if they haven't already, the more general categories that emerged through their webbing, such as "how dogs look" (appearance) and let them pull a few of these ideas together (e.g., fur, four legs, brown or blue eyes, tails, four legs). Think aloud, "Hmmm. So, if I were going to tell someone about dogs, one way I might give this information is to first talk about the way dogs look and tell all of the different features of a dog's appearance. That might become one heading in my presentation." Write *How Dogs Look* on the board.

5. Have students work in pairs to create some other headings and list the ideas under each heading. After a few minutes, discuss the different headings that were found.

6. Tell students that they have just organized their topic of dogs by description. Say, "You have taken a vast amount of information and put it into a more organized form that will be easier to identify what you know and what you don't know about your topic. You will probably not want to describe or know *everything* about your topic, but this procedure will help you identify some areas that you may want to describe. The next step will be to use the headings or some of the subheadings to develop good study questions. For example, you might decide that you want to know more about how dogs are trained or how

Organizing a Topic

animals communicate with one another. These can be turned into questions for your independent study."

7. Using the Student Booklet, have students identify the ways that they might want to describe their topic (see p. 16). Do they want to talk about their topic's contributions? People's feelings about it? Its future? How it works? Have students look at the webbing example on p. 17.

8. Have them spend a few minutes webbing what they know already about their own topics and what they might want to know using the ideas in the Student Booklet (see p. 18). If several have similar interests, they may work with each other to brainstorm ideas.

9. You may also want to bring in a few of the many nonfiction books that are organized by description and show how the author used headings with information and descriptions under each heading. Choose some books that are the same topic as the one you webbed in class.

10. After the students have webbed their own topics, have them share their webs and explore areas where they may have gaps in their knowledge. These areas become ripe for formulating questions.

11. Conclude the lesson by telling students that when they are studying a topic, they always will want to describe first, before they ask questions that compare their topic to other topics, look for causes or effects, or solve problems.

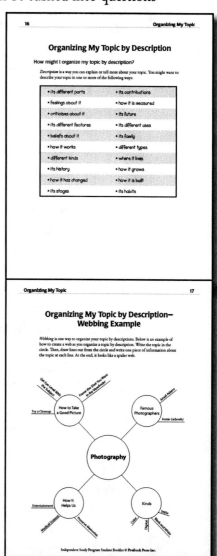

Lesson 3: Organizing by Comparisons

1. Write the word *compare* on the board. Ask students how they compare two things and what they actually do when they compare two things. For example, "What do you do when you compare dogs to cats?" Students may say they look for ways in which they are similar: both are animals; some are wild and some are pets; both have four legs, a tail, and fur; and the like. They should also look for ways in which they are different: eat different foods, make different sounds (purr vs. bark), cats climb trees, dogs are typically larger and heavier, and so on. Continue probing the students with questions such as, "What do you do when you compare World War I to World War II?" and "What do you do when you compare perspectives such as the use of a common language in the United States vs. multiple languages in other countries?"

2. Ask them to summarize or you can summarize by saying that they not only compared by similarities and differences, but that they also focused on several categories. Using the Student Booklet (see p. 20), make a similar table on the chalkboard or overhead. Select a few categories by which to compare the two animals, such as appearance, home, defense, what they eat, growth, how they communicate. Ask individuals or a group to fill in the information.

3. Have the students examine other topics and think about characteristics that they might compare. For example, when comparing famous athletes, they might think about their sport, their specialty, their background, their relative importance in their chosen sport, their future, their training history, and so on. (Notice how these categories may be developed from descriptions in the Student Booklet on p. 19.)

4. Next, have the students think about comparing their topic to a perfect model that may or may not

Organizing a Topic

even exist. Have them think about the "perfect athlete" or the "perfect pet." Suggest that the students might be interested in comparing their topic to a model, particularly if they are interested in building or creating something new. For example, a former students decided to compare the zoo's current habitat for Emperor Penguins with a model habitat and share this information with the zookeepers.

5. Now, have the students do a comparison on their own in their Student Booklet (see p. 20). Have them think about their topic and compare it to another topic or a model. Have them work independently or in small groups to identify characteristics for comparison and write what they know about the two topics. Have them share this information and note the areas that they need to learn more about. Point out that these gaps in knowledge will be useful in preparing their questions.

6. Conclude by asking, "What have you learned about making comparisons? Describe the process that you used when comparing two topics or a topic to a model. What might be some questions that you will want to ask in your study?"

Lesson 4: Organizing by Causes and Effects

1. Bring in books from the library or current events from newspapers or magazines that show changes or causes and effects. For example, you might want to bring in information on topics such as snakes, frogs, butterflies, life cycles, water forms, pollution, global warming, and space travel.

2. Tell students that when they look at causes and effects, they are really looking at the way something has changed. Write the word *change* on the board. Have students turn to the Causes and Effects section in the Student Booklet (see p. 21) that shows different types of change.

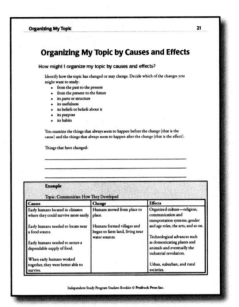

3. As a group, have students give examples of things that have changed. Jot their responses on the board. Possible examples might include babies to adults (i.e., humans, animals, insects, and so on); caterpillars to moths or butterflies; tadpoles to frogs; typewriting to word processing; polluted to clean environments; one-room schoolhouses to elementary, middle, and high schools; inventions that improved products; space travel; theories about how the solar system developed; and so on.

4. Now, look at the examples and discuss possible causes and effects for each change. Explain that *causes* mean the things that happen before the change that may help promote the change, and *effects* are the things that happen after the change that are related to the change.

Organizing a Topic

For example, water changes forms. What might be the causes and effects of water's change?

Cause	Change	Effect
warm temperature	water changes form	ice turns to water
hot temperature	water changes form	water changes to steam
cold temperature	water changes form	water turns to ice

Conclude by adding that most changes have many causes and many effects.

5. Have students look at the example in their Student Booklet (see p. 21). Say, "In this example, humans became less nomadic and began to live in communities. Some scientists believe that the climate, the environment, and ultimately survival were the causes that brought people together near water sources. Once people began living together in communities, many effects occurred—more organized cultures, technological advances, and the development of larger and different types of societies."

6. Using the Student Booklet (see p. 22), have the students write down some ideas of ways that their topic has changed. They might identify possible causes and effects independently, in pairs, and/or with a large- or small-group brainstorming session.

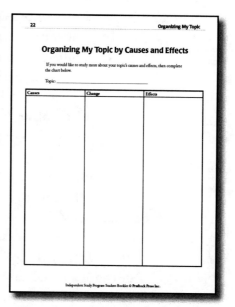

7. Have students tell what they know and don't know about the causes and effects of the change. What they don't know will help them formulate their questions.

8. Conclude by asking, "What have you learned about finding causes and effects? Describe the process that you used when identifying changes in your topic and possible causes and effects. What might be some questions that you will want to ask?"

Lesson 5: Organizing by Problems and Solutions

1. Write the word *problems* on the board. Have the students give examples of possible problems that have occurred at home or at school or that might relate to their topic. Write their responses on the board. Have the students look at their examples and discuss how they are alike and different. List these characteristics and have the students create a definition for the word problems.

2. Now, have the students look in their Student Booklet (see p. 23) and find how to organize their topics by problems and solutions. Have the students categorize their previous problems within the categories listed on p. 23 of the Student Booklet:
   - a difference between what is wanted and what is happening now,
   - a difference between what is happening now and what might happen in the future,
   - a difference between what is really happening and what is only imagined to be happening, and
   - what might happen in the future if a change does or doesn't happen.

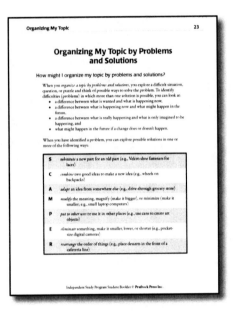

3. Have the students select one of the problems to solve. Have the students think of other problems that might relate to this problem. Write these new problems on the board. Now ask, "What is the biggest problem? If this problem were solved, would it solve all of the other problems?" Guide the students through this process by asking, "Would the answer to that problem solve this one?" Do this until the students have focused on a single problem.

4. Help the students elaborate the main problem by writing, "In what ways might _____" or "How might _____" solve the problem? For example, "In what ways might wildlife be managed so that animals and humans can coexist in a growing community?" Or, "How might we improve the disposal of trash in our school so that our school will consider conservation of resources?"

Organizing a Topic

5. Now, have the students break into small groups and identify possible solutions to the problem. Give each group 10 minutes to brainstorm at least 20 solutions. Remind the class about the brainstorming guides in Chapter 2: Selecting a Topic.

6. At the end of 10 minutes, ask each of the groups for the number of solutions that they were able to generate. Place the word SCAMPER on the board. Tell them that they are going to SCAMPER and think of even more solutions.

7. Have them look at p. 23 in their Student Booklets, which describes the SCAMPER strategy. Tell them that each letter in the word stands for a way of finding more solutions to the problem. Place the letter "S" on the board. Write the word *substitute* beside the letter. Tell the students to look at their solutions and substitute a *who* or a *what* in some of their solutions to produce at least five more solutions. Use one of the group's solutions to give them an example. Have the students substitute for 2 minutes.

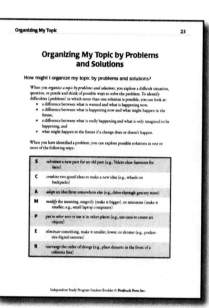

8. Now, place the letter "C" on the board. Write the word *combine* on the board. Tell the students to look at their solutions again and combine two or more of their solutions into one to produce at least five more solutions. Use one of the group's solutions to give them an example. Have the students combine for 2 more minutes.

9. Continue in this fashion using the SCAMPER techniques listed in the Student Booklet until all of the letters have been used. At the end of the process, have the students count the number of solutions that their group generated and share their best solutions with the entire class.

10. To conclude the problem-solving process, discuss how students might select the best solution for the problem. You might ask, "Which one would best relate to the problem?" "Which one is the most easily implemented?" "Which one is the most effective?" "Which one uses the least amount of resources?" and so on.

11. Now, have students discuss the problem-solving process that they used. What parts were easy? Which were difficult? What made them easy or difficult? What resources would have helped them? Did they have enough information to solve the problem?

12. Conclude by asking, "What have you learned about identifying problems and solutions? Describe the process that you used when identifying problems and solutions. Are you interested in identifying problems and solutions about your topic? What might be some questions that you will want to ask to identify problems? To identify solutions?"

Organizing a Topic

Ideas for Primary Students

- Young learners usually find that organizing by descriptions is the easiest way to arrange their information. They often will notice that many nonfiction books are organized by description. Using some nonfiction books as examples, point out the headings with information underneath that describes that topic. Encourage students to use headings as they collect information and to take notes about the topic underneath each heading.

- You may want to use the list of ways to organize a topic by description (see Student Booklet, p. 16) by turning the phrases in the Student Booklet into questions to guide the student's thinking. For example, you might say, "Do you want to know the different parts of an airplane?" "Do you want to know how it has changed?" "Do you want to know how it is built?" "Do you want to know people's feelings about flying?" and so on.

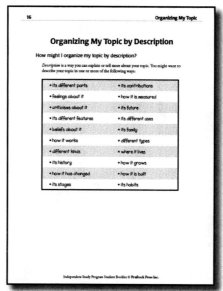

Tips for Teachers

- *Four methods.* There are four methods to organize a topic that were presented in this chapter: descriptions, comparisons, causes and effects, and problems and solutions. Generally, the easiest form of organizing research is by description. If this is the first study for students, you may want to teach this way to the entire group. Experienced researchers may branch out into more sophisticated ways of looking at material. It may work in your classroom to teach the other ways to organize topics to small groups as needed.

How might students ask questions to study?

- *Using question stems*—who, what, when, where, why, and how.
- *Asking higher level thinking questions*
- Little Thinking Questions are questions that can be answered by using known information.
- More Thinking Questions are questions that can be answered using already-known information in new situations.
- Most Thinking Questions are questions that create and/or evaluate new information.
- *Identifying and sequencing questions*
- Establish criteria for selection.
- Place in an order so that one question builds on the next.

Chapter 4 Overview

Chapter 4
Asking Questions

All the deep and true joys of the world
All the splendor and the mystery
Are within our reach.
—Ernest Hemingway

About Asking Questions

Children have a natural curiosity. Remember all of the questions young children ask just because they want to know the answers? "Why is the sky blue?" "What makes the light bulb glow?" "Why do the ocean waves roll so big?" "How did the mountain grow so tall?" Life is interesting with all of its wonders. One of our most important charges as teachers is to nurture the natural wondering of our students and help them to learn ways to answer the questions they have.

Questions, however, do need to be stimulated. We remember one time when we asked our middle school students what questions they might have for their independent studies—only to be confronted by silence. Knowing their curiosity, we decided that the students suddenly had no interest in asking questions when they became a part of an assignment. To avoid the problem, we decided to capture questions as they arose from genuine interests. We noticed that when our students studied a topic or a current issue, questions often arose. We placed these questions on a bulletin board or in a question box for future research possibilities. In this way, when we allotted time for independent research, many questions were available as a starting point.

Chapter 4 centers on encouraging students to ask questions that are a natural part of their curiosity. They wonder about their topics as they practice using stem words to generate a variety of questions and then select their most effective ones. We guide them to formulate questions that require higher level thinking as they begin to use old information in new ways or create new information. Finally, students sequence their questions in a logical order.

Objectives

1. The students will write questions to guide their study.
2. The students will organize and sequence questions for specific topics of study.

Key Concepts

- *Effective study questions*—A *question* is a request for information. A *study question* asks for information about a topic that students want to study. It has several distinct features:
    - is divergent, encouraging more than one possible answer;
    - requires plenty of time to study it;
    - has resources available to gather information about it; and
    - is useful or beneficial.

- *Stems for questions*—Guidewords, such as who, what, when, where, why, and how, that help students think of different types of information.
- *Sequence*—To arrange and organize questions in a logical order based on information needed to answer each of the questions.
- *Little Thinking Questions*—Use known information (Bloom's Revised taxonomy levels of Remember and Understand [Anderson et al., 2001]).
- *More Thinking Questions*—Use known information in new situations (Bloom's Revised taxonomy levels of Apply and Analyze [Anderson et al., 2001]).
- *Most Thinking Questions*—Create and/or evaluate new information (Bloom's Revised taxonomy levels of Evaluate and Create [Anderson et al., 2001]).

Materials for Teaching

- Resource Cards 15–19
- Student Booklets (pp. 24–30)

Evaluation Questions

1. Were the students able to write effective questions that
   - related to their topic,
   - might address the gaps in knowledge that they discovered when they organized their topic, and
   - are at a higher level of thinking?

2. Were the students able to group their questions in larger categories to identify broader questions?

3. Were the students able to sequence their questions from
   - Little to More to Most Thinking Questions and
   - from descriptive types of questions to more complex organization systems such as comparisons, causes and effects, and problems and solutions?

Lesson 1: Writing an Effective Study Question

1. Write the word *question* on the board. Ask, "What is a question?" Summarize their answers or say, "A question is a way to gather information. In this lesson, you are going to be learning about how to create good study questions for your independent study."

2. Connect to previous information by saying, "In the previous lesson, you discovered some new areas that you might want to study and some holes or gaps in what you knew or didn't know about your topic. You will now create questions to find the answers to the new or missing information. These questions will drive the rest of the study and determine the information that you will gather and the products that you will create. For example, let's assume that your topic is about eagles, and you have discovered that you don't know where eagles live. What might be a question that you would ask?" Have the students pose a question whose answer would address the eagle's habitat (e.g., "Where do eagles live?"). Have them notice that the question relates directly to the information that they will want to gather. Continue in this fashion using either the topic of eagles or their own topics. Be sure to include examples of effective study questions and ineffective study questions.

3. After the students have shared a variety of questions about eagles or their own topics, write *effective study questions* on the board. Say, "There are ways of asking effective study questions that help to guide independent research, and there are ineffective study questions that are not as helpful to you. Look at the qualities of an effective study question." Write on the board the following qualities of an effective study question:
    - is divergent, encouraging more than one possible answer;
    - requires plenty of time to study it;
    - has resources available to gather information about it; and
    - is useful or beneficial.

4. Have students look back at the questions they asked about eagles or their own topics. Help them find examples of effective study questions and discuss why the question fits the criteria of an effective study question.

Asking Questions

5. Review the eagle questions or those related to the students' topics and find one that is a ineffective study question that doesn't fit the criteria (e.g., How many kinds of eagles are there?). Discuss why it doesn't fit the criteria (i.e., it has only one answer that might be answered by looking in a book or visiting a Web site. Now, rework the question so that it *does* become a good study question (e.g., What are the types of eagles and how are they similar or different from one another? How is this type of classification system similar or different from other types of birds?). This process will take guidance from you to support the students' learning.

6. Pass out the Student Booklet and have the students turn to p. 24. Let the class decide which questions are effective study questions and which questions are ineffective study questions. Remember, an effective study question must meet all *four* criteria!

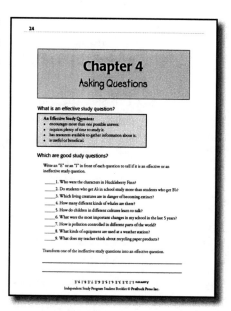

7. Using their Student Booklets (see p. 24), pair students and direct them to rework the ineffective study questions into effective study questions. Assign each pair a different question to revise. Let them post their before-and-after questions on a bulletin board or on the wall for future reference. Have the students describe how the initial question did not meet one or more of the criteria and how the new question meets all of the criteria.

Lesson 2: Using Stem Words to Write Study Questions

1. Connect to previous learning by saying, "In the previous lesson, you learned about how to construct and evaluate effective study questions. In this lesson, you will learn how to create more questions by using *stems*. Let's review some of the previous questions that you asked." Have the students review the ones that they created when they changed ineffective questions to more effective study questions. Have them notice the stems that they used. List these on the board and add additional stems to include all of the W's and the H (who, what, when, where, why, and how).

2. Tell the students that these words will help them think of different kinds of information about their topics and will also help in asking more questions. Have students turn to this section in their Student Booklets (p. 25) and fill out the chart with you following the instructions below.

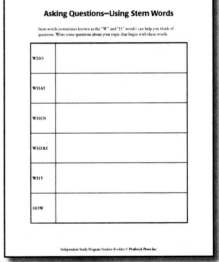

3. On the board, write a question beside the word *Who,* using a particular topic. For example, "Who studies seals?" Have the students think about their topics and write a question beside the word *Who* in their Student Booklets. Have them share their examples with the class, in small groups, or in pairs.

4. On the board, write a question beside the word *What*. For example, "What does a seal look like? What environment is best for seals? What kinds of seals are there? What do people use sealskins for? What do seals do?" Have the students think about their topics and write a question beside the word *What* in their Student Booklets. Have them share their examples with the class, in small groups, or in pairs.

Asking Questions

5. Continue in this manner until the students have used each of the stems to write questions about their topic. Use Resource Card 16 in this section for more questions about seals.

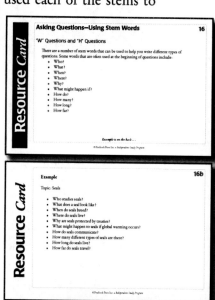

6. Examine all of the questions that you have written on the board and have students decide which ones are effective study questions and which ones are not. As a group, change the ineffective study questions into effective study questions using the criteria. Next, have students review the questions that they have written about their topics in the Student Booklet. Have them share their effective questions with the class, in small groups, or in pairs.

7. Conclude by asking, "What have you learned about creating questions? Describe the process that you used when you created questions. Which ones do you think that you will use for your independent study? Why?"

Lesson 3: Asking Higher Level Questions

1. Tell the students that they are going to learn how to ask questions that are more complex and that allow them to think more deeply about their topics.

   Say, "They are frequently called higher level thinking questions. These questions may be divided into three broad categories." Have the students open their Student Booklet to Asking Higher Level Questions on p. 26. (Note: For older students, you might want to teach them the name for each level of Bloom's Revised taxonomy—Little Thinking [Remember and Understand], More Thinking [Apply and Analyze], Most Thinking [Evaluate and Create].)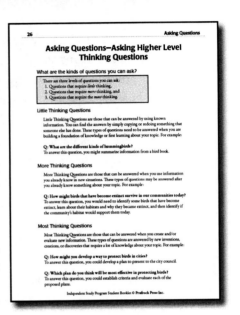

2. Tell students, "The first category of questions that I will describe is Little Thinking Questions." Write on the board the words *Little Thinking Questions*. Beside the words, write the following definition: "Questions that require little thinking are those that can be answered by simply copying or redoing something that someone else has done. Researchers (Anderson et al., 2001) who study thinking would consider these types of questions to be those that ask us to *remember* and *understand*."

   Say, "This type of question is needed when you are building a foundation of knowledge or first learning about your topics. For example: 'What are the different kinds of seals? Where do seals live? What are the different kinds of hummingbirds?' They are described as 'Little Thinking' because most of the information can be gathered from looking in books or on the Internet."

3. Write on the board the words *More Thinking Questions*. Beside the words, write the following definition: "Questions that require more thinking are those that can be answered when you use information you already know in new situations. Researchers (Anderson et al., 2001) would consider these types of questions as those that ask us to *apply* and *analyze*."

   Say, "For example: 'How might you teach other students about birds? (The new situation is teaching what you know to others.) How might that

Asking Questions

have become extinct survive in our communities today? (The new situation is taking something from the past and placing it in the present.) How might global warming affect the survival of birds?' (The new situation is taking something from the present and projecting it into the future.) This type of question is asked after you already know some information about your topic. You then must use the information you know in a new situation."

4. Write on the board the words *Most Thinking Questions*. Beside the words, write the following definition: "Questions that require most thinking are those that can be answered only if you evaluate or create new information. Researchers (Anderson et al., 2001) would consider these types of questions to be those that ask us to *evaluate* and *create*."

   Say, "For example: 'How might you develop a way to protect birds in cities? Which of these plans do you think will be most effective in protecting birds?' This type of question is asked when you are interested in creating something new or using new criteria to evaluate something that is known or something new."

5. Have the students check their understanding of the three types of question categories by completing pp. 27–28 in their Student Booklets independently. Then, have the students share their responses in small groups. Have them discuss the characteristics that influenced their decisions and the methods that they used in developing questions. If there are any differences of opinion regarding the category, have the students share these with the rest of the group and discuss. (Possible answers for Raising the Level of Questions on p. 28 include: (1) How are your reading preferences similar or different than your classmates? (2) How does the size of a state influence its power within the United States? (3) What might happen to the world's climate if rain forests were destroyed? (4) How are bone structures in the human body similar or different to other animal species?)

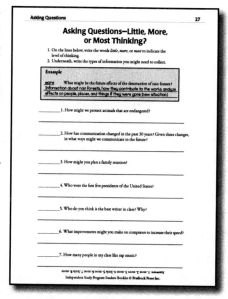

6. If you believe that the students understand the various types of questions, have them write study questions for their own topic on p. 29 in the Student Booklet.

7. Conclude by having the students share their study questions with one another, summarizing the characteristics of the various categories of questions.

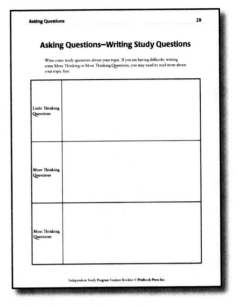

Lesson 4: Organizing and Sequencing Questions for Study

1. Tell the students that because they have developed a number of interesting questions about their topic, they are ready to organize and sequence them to begin their research. Ask one of the students to share the questions for his or her independent study with the class. List these on the board.

2. Ask, "Which questions will you be able to answer by using known information?" Have the students find the Little Thinking Questions and place them first in the sequence. Ask, "Why do you think you will answer these questions first?" The students might respond that you answer these first when you are learning about your topic and building a foundation of knowledge. Then ask, "Which ones will you ask next?" The students will then place the More and Most Thinking Questions next in the sequence.

3. If the students have a long list of questions, you might want to help them organize their questions into categories. First, have the students notice how the questions are alike or different. For example, some of the questions may relate to how the topic looks, whereas others may relate to how the topic is used. This process may reduce the number of questions for the students to research.

4. Students might want to further reduce the number of questions in their study by reviewing the criteria on p. 30 in their Student Booklets.
    - Which questions do I have resources for?
    - Which questions might I answer within the time that I have?
    - Which questions are the most interesting to me?
    - Which questions are most beneficial?
    - Which questions require the most thinking?

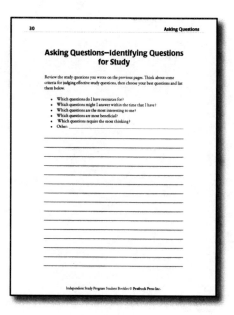

At the end of this evaluation, have the students list their study questions on p. 30 in their Student Booklets.

Ideas for Primary Students

- The younger grades are an ideal time to teach students that good research stems from asking questions. Children are naturally curious and we encourage them to ask many questions about their topics. For example, if a child has selected the topic of *tigers* to study, ask, "What do you want to know about tigers?" (e.g., How big do they get? Where do they live? How fast can they run? What do they eat? How many babies do they have?) There are many wonderful nonfiction books that present information in a question/answer format that can be used as a model for young writers. Later, as they develop skill in developing stem questions, you will want to teach them how to develop higher level thinking questions.

- As students gather information by reading or listening to books, conducting experiments, or observing the natural environment, they may answer some of the questions they asked, but they will also find many more interesting facts that they haven't asked questions about. Afterward, guide them to ask other questions that they learned facts about as they were gathering information.

Tips for Teachers

- *Background information.* We have found that students need background information on their topics before they are able to ask effective study questions. Initially, they may develop some tentative questions, gather information, and then return to their questions to refine or add new ones. This process is ongoing as the students learn to develop more and more effective questions.

- *Changing topics.* Do not be dismayed if at this point, or even a later point, the students decide to change their topics. It's not unusual for students to select a topic quickly and then discover as they learn more that it is not as interesting to them as it was in the beginning. Allow them to make changes so that they are engaged in their independent study. You might, however, need to identify a final deadline for selecting a topic for those who tend to have difficulty making a decision.

- *Balance of questions.* Remind students that Little Thinking Questions are not poor questions. Students need to answer the Little Thinking Questions to build the knowledge so that they can answer the More and Most Thinking Questions. The independent study will need a balance of questions. We suggest that for a student's first independent study, it is best to have only one or two More and Most Thinking Questions because they take more time to research.

- *Sequencing questions.* Questions may be sequenced in a variety of ways—from the W's to higher level thinking questions, or from descriptions to problems and solutions. The students need to consider if the knowledge from one question will help answer the next question in the sequence.

Chapter 5 Overview

How does the student match a study method to the questions?

- *Action study*—Examining an improvement that is made to solve a problem.
- *Case study*—Observing closely a person, animal, group, system, or thing.
- *Correlation study*—Relating one thing to another thing using numbers.
- *Descriptive study*—Describing something with numbers or facts.
- *Developmental study*—Observing the development of or changes in a topic.
- *Experimental study*—Conducting an experiment and looking carefully at the results.
- *Factual study*—Collecting facts about something.
- *Historical study*—Analyzing the past or history of a topic.

Chapter 5
Using a Study Method

The function of intelligence is not to copy but to invent.
—J. H. Rush

About Using a Study Method

Amanda was interested in glyptodonts. She had seen this ancient armadillo in the natural history museum and had become fascinated with this animal ever since she was 4 years old. Now, at 5 and in kindergarten, she was eager to conduct her research on this topic. Because she was an early reader, her kindergarten teacher gathered some books together on glyptodonts and showed Amanda the index, the table of contents, and how to collect factual information about her topics. Using a matrix on a large sheet of paper, the teacher placed Amanda's questions on the left-hand side of the page. At the top, he listed the books that Amanda planned on reading. He told Amanda to look in the books and find out what each book said about her questions.

The teacher took Amanda's first question—"What do glyptodonts eat?"—and showed her how to find the information about that question in each of the books. Together, they wrote the answer in each cell next to the question and under the name of the book where they found the answer. The teacher was showing Amanda how to collect factual information and how to compare information across sources. Amanda was delighted to learn about this way of collecting information and began reading her books and writing down the information next to her questions.

The next day, as the teacher drove into the parking lot, he noticed Amanda running towards his car—waving two books in her hands. As the teacher lowered his car window, Amanda peeped in and exclaimed loudly, "This book spells glyptodont with a 't' and this one does not!" The teacher shared Amanda's excitement and declared that Amanda was becoming a scientist—learning how to collect factual information. Amanda learned that books are not always correct.

As this story suggests, even very young children use a study method when they are learning about their topics. In Amanda's case, she was learning how to collect factual information from several sources to triangulate her data. In this chapter, the students will be learning about a variety of study methods: factual, descriptive, historical, developmental, case study, correlation, action, and experimental. Your job as the teacher will be to help the students in finding the best study method for the questions they have asked about their topics.

Objectives

1. The students will select study methods that match their questions.
2. The students will use the steps needed to gather information about their topics.

Key Concepts

- *Method*—A systematic way of doing something according to an organized plan.
- *Action study*—Examining an improvement that is made to solve a problem.
- *Case study*—Observing closely a person, animal, group, system, or thing.
- *Correlation study*—Relating one thing to another thing using numbers.
- *Descriptive study*—Describing something with numbers or facts.
- *Developmental study*—Observing the development of or changes in a topic.
- *Experimental study*—Conducting an experiment and looking carefully at the results.
- *Factual study*—Collecting facts about something.
- *Historical study*—Analyzing the past or history of a topic.

Materials for Teaching

- Resource Cards 20–38
- Student Booklets (pp. 31–33)

Evaluation Questions

1. Did the students select study methods that matched their questions?
2. Were the students able to write or tell the steps needed to gather information about their questions?

Lesson 1: Selecting Study Methods to Match Questions

1. Have students open their Student Booklets to the Chapter 5: Using a Study Method section (see p. 31). Read the definition at the top of the page: "A study method describes certain steps that you will follow when you study your questions."

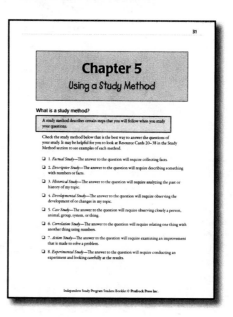

2. Tell students, "A study method is similar to a recipe that you might follow when preparing a specific dish." Have a simple recipe with the ingredients needed to create the final product (e.g., a sandwich). Talk aloud as you make the sandwich and note how closely you are following the recipe. Be sure that you measure each ingredient carefully—four slices of lunchmeat, one piece of lettuce, two tomatoes, one half teaspoon of mustard, etc.. Now, have a student volunteer make the sandwich exactly like yours. After making the two sandwiches, ask the students, "What helped us make the sandwich in the same way? Do you think that the two sandwiches will taste the same?"

3. Tell students that scientists are just like cooks in a kitchen. Say, "They follow a systematic set of steps like a recipe when they study a question or a problem. In this way, other scientists can do the same thing and see if they get the same results. This is called *replication*. Replication is important in science because it tells us if something really works or if it was just luck that it worked the first time—in other words, it works over and over again instead of just one time. In the case of the sandwich, if it tastes good the first time, it should taste good the next time if the cook followed a specific procedure or method."

4. When scientists choose a particular method to use, they match it to the types of questions they are asking. Have students look at the study methods that are listed in their Student Booklet on p. 31. Read the statement that is next to *factual study*.

5. Tell the students that everyone will be collecting factual information. Discuss how to gather factual information, using Resource Cards 21–22. Show them a chart similar to the one on the Resource Card 22b. Place these questions on each row in the chart:

    - How many students are in our school?
    - How many are girls?
    - How many are boys?
    - How many are new to the school this year?

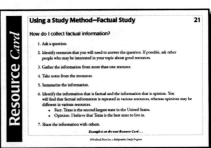

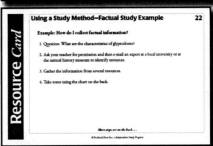

At the top of the chart, list three students: Student #1, Student #2, and Student #3. Leave room at the top of the chart to fill in additional columns of information. Now, ask three volunteer students the four questions, and fill in their answers. Ask the rest of the class if this information is factual. Is it nonbiased? Then ask students what other sources they could use to gather this information (e.g., the principal, the attendance clerk, the school's Web site). Add these sources to the top of the chart and tell the class that it would be important to also check these sources to find the answers to the four questions. Describe for the students what biased and nonbiased sources of information might be. Explain how a nonbiased sample might be selected using Resource Card 38. Ask the students if the three students might be biased or nonbiased.

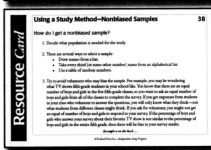

6. Ask students to think of "good" and nonbiased sources of information. You might have the students describe their topics and share their ideas for some possible sources. Have the students evaluate their own sources by asking, "Does it relate to your topic? Does it relate to your questions? Will it have factual information and not try to sell you something or tell you something that would favor the source?"

7. Now, ask the students what they have learned about collecting factual information. Students should mention that it is important to find more than one source of information.

Lesson 2: Using One Method to Answer Specific Questions

1. Review with the students the factual study method that they learned in the previous lesson. Tell them that they are going to learn about other study methods available for answering their specific questions. Have them look at the other methods in the Student Booklet on p. 31. Briefly describe each of these methods.

2. Have the students turn to the next page in the Student Booklet (see p. 32) and match the study methods to the questions. Discuss their answers. Point out the characteristics of any of the methods that they might have missed. For example, if they confuse descriptive study with a factual study, remind them that a descriptive study requires summarizing information with numbers, whereas a factual study uses words.

3. Put students into groups according to which method best matches their study questions and pass out the corresponding Resource Cards (see the Tips for Teachers section on p. 95). Now have the students turn to p. 33 in their Student Booklets and identify the method and steps for their study. Conclude by saying that you will be helping each of the groups use the steps listed on the Resource Cards. Each study method is described below.

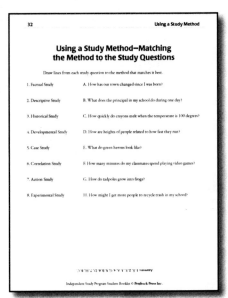

Descriptive Study

1. This kind of study may be used when students ask a question that requires them to *describe something with numbers or facts.*

2. Explain that students might gather information in the form of surveys, questionnaires, interviews, observations, test scores, and records.

Using a Study Method

3. Guide students whose questions might be studied using the descriptive study method to follow these steps. Students should:
    - Ask a question that can be answered with numbers or facts.
    - Decide if they are going to use information that is already known or get new information. Note: If they are collecting new information, make sure that the information is objective. Do this by identifying persons who represent the population and identify an observation or data collection method that tries to collect nonbiased information.
    - Collect old information in books, magazines, newspapers, movies, TV shows, DVDs, the Internet, and so forth.
    - Get new information by doing interviews, surveys, or experiments.
    - Develop a form to collect data (e.g., numbers or information).
    - Gather the information.
    - Identify which information is based on facts and which information is based on opinion.
    - Summarize the notes.
    - Present the information to other people.

4. Present a sample question, such as "In our grade, what is the average amount of time students use computers each day?" and model how you might answer this question using the steps listed in #3 or use the example on Resource Card 24.

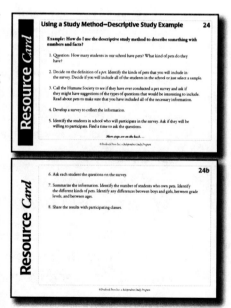

Historical Study

1. This study method might be used when students ask a question that requires them to look at the *past or history* of their topic.

2. Explain that information might be gathered by interviews, primary sources, letters, notes from historical books or records, and the like.

3. Guide students whose questions might be studied using the historical study method to follow these steps. Students should:

- Ask a question that can be answered by looking at the past or history of the topic.
- Look for both primary and secondary sources. In primary sources, the author has directly observed the historical event. In secondary sources, the author reports the observations of others who witnessed the event.
- Collect information from various resources, such as people who observed the historical event, historians at colleges, historical societies, museums, old documents and records, books, the Internet, magazines and newspapers, encyclopedias, movies, and TV shows.
- Take notes from the resources.
- Examine the resources and notes. Make sure that the resources are authentic (students should ask themselves whether the author would have a motive or a bias to exaggerate, distort, or overlook information).
- Decide which information is based on facts and which information is based on opinion.
- Summarize the notes.
- Present the information to other people. Students should include the names of all of the resources they used and tell how they decided whether or not they were authentic.

4. Present a sample question, such as "How did the different schools in our town get their names?" and model how you might answer this question using the steps listed in #3 or Resource Card 26.

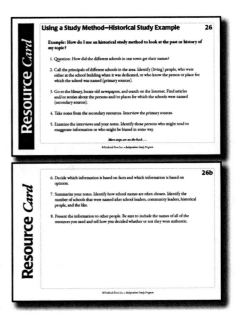

Developmental Study

1. Students may use a developmental study when they ask questions in which they notice the *change or development* of a topic over time.

2. Explain that information might be collected by observations, questionnaires, tests, interviews, letters, library or Internet research, and the like.

Using a Study Method

3. Guide students whose questions might be studied using the developmental study method to follow these steps. Students should:
   - Ask a question that can be answered by studying the change or development of a topic over time.
   - Examine how other people have looked at a change in or development of the topic in the past.
   - Find how others have looked at change by interviewing experts; writing letters or e-mail messages to others who are interested in the topic; and reading books, magazines, newspapers, journals, encyclopedias, or Internet sites.
   - Design a way that the student will observe the changes or development of the topic.
   - Study the changes or development by giving a test or questionnaire at the beginning and at the end of the study, or observe something every day and chart or graph the information. Then, students can notice the changes that have occurred.
   - Collect the data.
   - Summarize the data.
   - Present the information to other people.

4. Present a sample question, such as "What are my classmates' attitudes toward school throughout the year? Do they change or remain the same?" and model how you might answer this question using the steps listed in #3 or Resource Card 28.

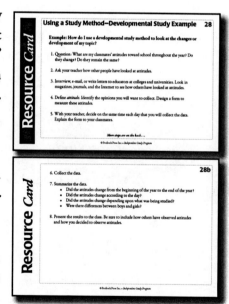

Case Study

1. This kind of study might be used when students closely *observe a person, group, place, or thing*.

2. Discuss that methods to collect information might include interviewing, observing, tape recording, videotaping, and taking notes.

3. Guide students whose questions might be studied using the case study method to follow these steps. Students should:

- Ask a question that can be answered by closely observing a person, group, place, or thing.
- Examine how other people have looked at a person, group, place, or thing.
- Find how others have looked at the particular person, group, place, or thing by interviewing experts; writing letters or e-mail messages to others who are interested in the topic; or reading books, magazines, newspapers, journals, encyclopedias, or Internet sites.
- Find a person (or group of people) who is willing to let students observe him or her. If students are going to observe a place or thing, they must locate it and get permission to observe it.
- Design a way to observe the person, group, place, or thing. Plan how long to observe and how to take notes (e.g., using a tape recorder, video recorder, DVD, journal, or note cards).
- Collect the data by observation.
- Summarize the data.
- Present the information to other people. Students should tell them why they decided to observe this person, group, place, or thing; how they conducted the study; and what was learned.

4. Present a sample question, such as "How does a principal spend his or her time during the school day?" and model how you might answer this question using the steps listed in #3 or Resource Card 30.

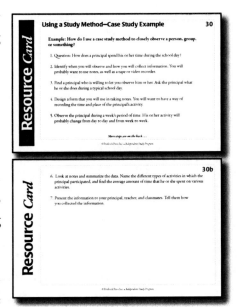

Correlation Study

1. This study method might be used when students ask a question that requires them to compare one thing with another thing using numbers.

2. Talk about how information might be collected through interviews, observations, tape recordings, notes, tests, surveys, readings, census reports, and the Internet.

Using a Study Method

3. Guide students whose questions might be studied using the correlation study method to follow these steps. Students should:
   - Ask a question that requires them to compare one thing with another thing using numbers.
   - Describe each thing that they are comparing. Study how others have described these things and how they have measured or studied them.
   - Decide what or who will be in the study. Select a sample that represents the general population and is not biased.
   - Plan how they will measure each thing that will be compared: Will students look at tests? Will they observe how something grows? Will they get information from newspapers or the Internet?
   - Collect the data.
   - Put the data about one item on a line graph. Put the data about the other item on a separate line graph (or a separate line on the same graph). Compare the two items.
   - Analyze the data on the graph. If the two lines go up or down in the same way (e.g., they are parallel), the items are related. This means when one item occurs, the other will probably happen. If one line goes down and one line goes up, the items are *inversely* related. This means when one item occurs, the other will probably *not* happen. Finally, if the lines don't look like either of the two previously described ways, the items are probably not related.
   - Share the information with other people.

4. Present a sample question, such as "Is there a relationship between the number of study hours at home and grades?" and model how you might answer this question using the steps listed in #3 or Resource Card 32.

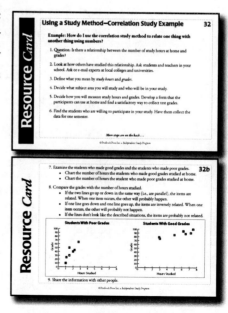

Action Study

1. An action study might be used when students ask a question that allows them to examine an *improvement they made to solve a problem.*

2. Tell students that information might be collected through interviews, observations,

training programs, experiments, tests, surveys, readings, Internet research, and the like.

3. Guide students whose questions might be studied using the action study method to follow these steps. Students should:
   - Ask a question that can be answered by looking at an improvement made to solve a problem.
   - Identify a problem that needs to be solved.
   - Find information about how others have solved this problem. Students should contact experts at colleges, businesses, or chambers of commerce; look at readings such as books, magazines, newspapers, journals, and Internet resources; and watch TV shows or DVD documentaries.
   - Take notes from the resources.
   - Decide how the problem might be solved.
   - Plan how to measure whether or not the improvement changes the problem. For example, it might be tested at the beginning and at the end, or it might be graphed each day.
   - Get permission from everyone who will be involved in the study.
   - Collect the data.
   - Record and analyze the results.
   - Present the information to other people.

4. Present a sample question, such as "How can we reduce the noise in the cafeteria?" and model how you might answer this question using the steps listed in #3 or Resource Card 34.

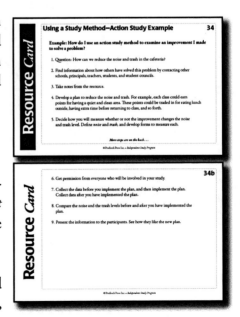

Experimental Study

1. This study method might be used when students ask a question that requires them to *set up and conduct an experiment* and look at the results.

2. Explain that information might be gathered by interviews, observations, tests, surveys, readings, and the like.

Using a Study Method

3. Guide students whose questions might be studied using the experimental study method to follow these steps. Students should:
   - Ask a question that can be answered by looking look at one thing (i.e., a variable) that may be changing while controlling other things (i.e., other variables).
   - Describe each variable that is going to be in the experiment.
   - Look at how others have described these variables and how they have measured or studied them.
   - Decide what or who will be in the study and remember to select a sample that represents the general population and is not biased.
   - Decide how to measure the variables.
   - Select a research design.
   - Conduct the experiment.
   - Summarize the data. Use graphs, charts, and/or tables to show the data.
   - Present the information to other people.

4. Present a sample question such as "Does memorizing lists of words help students to spell similar words when writing sentences?" and model how you might answer this question using the steps listed in #3 or Resource Card 36.

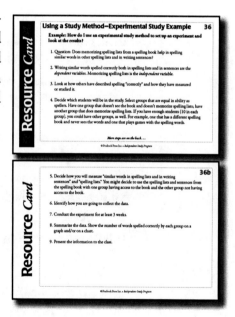

Ideas for Primary Students

- When working with young students, use methods that are more hands-on. For example, if a student wants to study about the characteristics of crayons, set up experiments that allow him or her to see how the properties of crayons change in different settings (e.g., in the freezer, in direct heat, outside on the sidewalk, in the classroom, and so on).

- Young students also enjoy doing descriptive studies. Using surveys, they are eager to discover their classmate's answers to questions such as the number and types of pets that their classmates own. This information can be compiled simply using bar graphs.

Tips for Teachers

- *Use one method.* With initial studies, you may want to have all of the students ask questions that require only one method of study—for example, descriptive. In this way, you can teach a single method to the class initially before the students branch into other methods during future independent studies.

- *Work with small groups.* Group students according to the method you think is appropriate for their questions. To save time, you might peruse their Student Booklets the day before to see what study questions they are asking. Decide which study method would be the best match to answer their questions. Then, work with the small groups. Other students may collect information while you are helping each group.

- *Guide students how to select.* As students progress through several independent studies, they will begin to understand how to select the study method themselves. It may involve guiding them through the process of how to select the appropriate method during the first independent study.

Chapter 6 Overview

What information sources are available to answer students' questions?

- Internet
- electronic sources
- objects/materials for experiments
- people
- places
- print/text

In what ways can students collect information?

- conducting an experiment
- corresponding by letter or e-mail
- interviewing
- observing
- reading
- searching the Internet
- conducting a survey

How can students organize information?

- classifying
- outlining
- summarizing
- taking notes
- using index cards
- webbing

Chapter 6
Collecting Information

Some books are to be tasted, others to be swallowed, and some few to be chewed and digested.
—F. Bacon

About Collecting Information

With so much virtual information at the touch of a computer key, in the process of collecting information students need to learn how to discern facts from opinions, bias from balanced reporting, and sources that provide credible information from those trying to sell a particular idea or product. Ultimately, the students will need to relate their information to their questions and understand the connections among facts, concepts, generalizations, principles, and theories. For example, Stan, a fifth grader, was an avid video game player and science fiction fan. He'd read about time warps, interplanetary space travel, meteors, and doomsday predictions. Through these experiences, he had decided that he wanted to study black holes, worm holes, and white holes. These were theoretical concepts that Stan treated as truly existing in the real universe. I guided Stan in his study by having him read a variety of books on astronomy and interview experts. Using the method for collecting factual information, he soon discovered that his topics were theoretical, and scientists had different opinions about the fabric of the universe. I encouraged him to create his own theory based on his reading and his interviews, which he enthusiastically developed. His final product astounded his peers and parents. He had carefully described the hypothetical characteristics of black holes, worm holes, and white holes, adding the shape of the universe as an important underlying context. He then explained his theory and how it related to other current theories. How amazing students are when they learn how to pursue their topics of interest!

This chapter launches students into various ways of gathering information to answer their study questions. With the Internet, the entire world is literally at our fingertips and children can learn early how to access information and experts. School and public libraries contain many well-written factual and nonfiction books for children of all levels that make learning enjoyable and doable. With so much information available, sometimes it can be overwhelming. This chapter helps to guide students to the various resources that are available and to provide ways to organize the vast amounts of information that they find.

Objectives

1. The students will examine various ways to collect information about their questions.
2. The students will select and use several ways to collect information.

Key Concepts

- *Collecting information*—Acquiring knowledge and gathering facts and data about a topic.
- *Sources*—People, places, or things (e.g., Internet, books) that provide the information.
- *Methods*—Ways of collecting information from the sources.
- *Organizing*—Ways of keeping records of the information that has been collected.

Materials for Teaching

- Resource Cards 39–72
- Internet access
- E-mail
- Student Booklets (pp. 34–36)
- Resources that might be useful for the students' studies

Evaluation Questions

1. Did the students use different sources for collecting information?
2. Did the students use different methods for collecting information?
3. Did the students use a method for organizing the information they collected?

Collecting Information

Lesson 1: Examining Ways of Collecting Information

1. Have students open their Student Booklets to Chapter 6: Collecting Information. Tell them, "Before you can gather information about a topic, you need to know how to get the information. Let's think about all of the various resources you can use to answer your questions about your topics." As a group, discuss and write their ideas on the board. These ideas might include books; Internet; magazines (they may even list specific magazines, such as *Discover*, *Smithsonian*, and others); newspapers; interviews (this might be in person or by phone, e-mail, or letter); letters; encyclopedias; television documentaries; videos/DVDs; radio interviews; reference books; field trips; experiments; guest speakers; and so on.

2. Mention that these resources may be classified within two categories: who or what you get the information from—the source—and how you get the information—the method.

3. Place the following matrix on the board and have the students classify their ideas under each of the two categories. Have the students connect the different methods to the sources by drawing lines. Discuss how you might use one source in several ways. For example, you might visit the Internet to locate experts to interview or materials to read.

Source (Who or What)	Method (How)

4. Ask, "Why do you think it's important to use more than one source of information?" Students might respond that different writers may have different knowledge and opinions; different books may focus on specific aspects of a topic; there may be different information in each source; and it is important to make sure they find factual information.

5. Now, have the students examine the various methods of collecting information from their sources. If not already listed, guide them to include the following:
    - conducting an experiment,
    - corresponding by letter or e-mail,
    - interviewing,
    - observing,
    - reading,
    - searching the Internet, and
    - conducting a survey. (See Resource Cards 54–60 for more detailed information.)

    Point out that they may not use all of these ways to gather information from their sources, but they will want to use as many as needed to answer their questions. The choice is theirs.

6. Within this overview of collecting information, finally mention that once the students have collected their information, they will need to organize it in some way to make it manageable. List these ways of organizing information at the bottom of the chart you've already started filling out: classifying, outlining, summarizing, taking notes, using index cards, and webbing.

Source (Who or What)	Method (How)
Organizing Information: classifying, outlining, summarizing, taking notes, using index cards, webbing	

7. Say, "I'm going to show you a way of collecting information to answer a question using specific sources, a method for getting information from the source, and an organization approach." Present an example of how you might select several resources for a topic such as *wolves*. Bring in several sources on the topic you choose to show them the different kinds of information you may obtain from each one. Remember to *show* (don't just tell) them how you might find the sources, select the methods, and organize some of the information you found.

    Say, "I want to find information to answer these two questions: What are the different kinds of wolves?" and "How do wolves communicate?" To find the information I'm looking for, I might look at these sources:

Collecting Information

- *Wolves* by Seymour Simon and other books on this topic,
- an interview of someone who works at a wildlife reserve (a list of questions and notes of the person's answers),
- a documentary video on wolves from library,
- a DVD encyclopedia entry, and
- an Internet address with printout (e.g., http://www.wolveswolveswolves.org)."

On an overhead transparency, board, or large chart paper, list different ways to organize the information (see Figure 7 for an example).

8. Summarize this lesson by asking the students these questions:
   - What are sources of information?
   - What are methods for collecting information?
   - What are ways of organizing information?
   - Compare and contrast sources, methods for collecting information from the sources, and ways of organizing information.

Tell the students to begin thinking about the sources and the ways that they might want to collect information to answer their specific study questions.

Ways to Organize Information Collected	Example of How to Organize Information Using the Topic of Wolves

Classifying	Types of Wolves:
	    Gray
	    Red
	    Ethiopian
	    Maned
	
	Wolves' Communication:
	    Sound
	    Body Language

Outlining	Wolves
	    I. Types of Wolves
	        A. Gray
	        B. Red
	        C. Ethiopian
	        D. Maned
	
	    II. Ways Wolves Communicate
	        A. Sound
	            1. growl
	            2. yelp
	            3. bark
	            4. howl
	        B. Body Language
	            1. leader holds tail straight up
	            2. bares teeth when angry
	            3. young wolves lie down in front of older wolves

Summarizing	Wolves communicate in two different ways: the sounds they make and the body language they use. They make sounds by growling, yelping, barking, and howling. These sounds can tell other wolves a lot, such as where they are, if there is danger or prey, and if they are happy or distressed. Body language can say something silently. Wolves can see that the leader holds up a straight tail and the leader is angry when he bares his teeth. They show respect by lying on the ground in front of an older wolf. Specific sounds and body language help wolves communicate with each other.

Taking Notes	Notes about the ways wolves communicate (from *Endangered! Wolves* by Casey Horton):
	
	• growling, yelping, barking, and howling
	• each wolf howls on a different note
	• body language
	    • leader holds tail straight up
	    • bares teeth to show anger
	    • young wolves lie on ground in front of older wolves

Webbing	Different Notes, Growling, Body Language — Communication — Wolves — Kinds — Gray, Red, Ethiopian, Maned

Figure 7. Examples of ways to organize information.

Lesson 2: Collecting Information to Answer Specific Questions

1. Have the students provide definitions and at least one example of possible sources, methods for collecting information, and ways of organizing information. Say, "Today, you are going to identify specific sources, methods, and ways of organizing to answer your specific study questions."

2. Have students open their Student Booklets to Chapter 6: Collecting Information (see p. 34). Tell the students that they will have an opportunity to describe the sources of information that they will use to answer their questions. Have one of the students read the directions and the example. Have other students provide some possible examples. Next, have each of the students write down a few examples of resources they think would be useful for answering their own study questions in their Student Booklets.

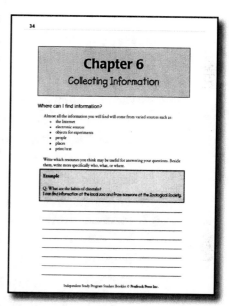

3. Have the students share the examples that they have written, elaborating as needed to include the question and fully addressing who, what, and where. Have each student also describe why he or she decided to select that source. Add the following questions as criteria for making a decision about sources, "Will the source provide information about your question? Is it a unbiased source of information? What other sources might you use to answer the question to ensure that you have factual information?"

4. Have the students take one of the sources that they have identified and look at Using Varied Methods in the Student Booklet (see p. 35). Have one of the students read the directions and the example. Have him or her notice how the interview directly relates to the question about the topic. Now, have the students write several ways that they will collect information

from a source that they listed on the previous page of the Student Booklet. Remind them to be specific about the information that they hope to gather.

5. Have the students share the examples that they have written, elaborating as needed to include the question, the source, and what information they hope to gather. Have the students also describe why they decided to select that method. Add these questions as criteria for making a decision about the method, "Will the method provide information about your question? Is it an unbiased method for collecting information? What other methods might you use to answer the question to ensure that you have factual information?"

6. Have the students turn to p. 36 in their Student Booklets and describe ways of organizing their information. If possible, share some examples of ways that previous students have organized information for their independent studies. Next, have a student read the directions and the example. Have the students write how they plan to organize their own studies.

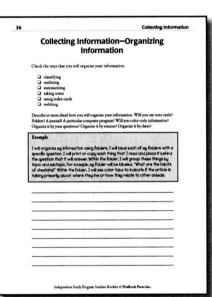

7. Have the students share the examples that they have written, elaborating how they will organize their information by questions, topics, and subtopics. Have the students also describe why they decided on a particular organization method. Add these questions as criteria for making a decision about the method, "How will the method help you locate information when you need it? How will it help organize information about specific questions and subtopics?"

8. Summarize by saying that the students have identified some sources, ways of collecting information, and ways of organizing information. Place a chart on the board with these categories and have the students write or place a sticky note under the source, method for collecting information, and the way of organizing information that they plan to use (see Figure 8).

Collecting Information

Source					
Internet	Electronic	Objects	People	Places	Print/Text
Sam Maria			Jessica Robert		James
Method					
Experiment	Letter/E-mail	Interview	Observe	Read	Internet	Survey
	Robert	Jessica		James	Sam Maria	
Organize					
Classify	Outline	Summarize	Take Notes	Index Cards	Webs
	James	Sam Robert	Maria Jessica		

Figure 8. Example of organizing information chart.

9. Form small instructional groups around specific methods and pass out the corresponding Resource Cards. (Note that collecting information by conducting experiments will be found on Resource Card 35.) Conclude by saying that you will be helping each of the groups use the steps that are listed on Resource Cards 39–72.

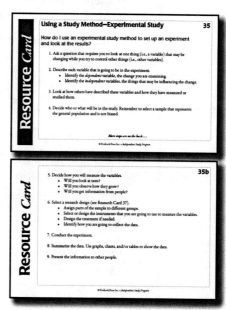

Ideas for Primary Students

- Have primary students use ways of collecting and organizing information that limit the amount of writing, such as conducting a survey, interviewing, observing, and conducting experiments. Early readers will also enjoy books, but they might wish to organize the information by telling a more able writer about the book or by dictating it to you.

- Gathering information from books may be new for young readers, so you may want to preview the books and mark relevant pages with sticky notes that are color-coded to specific questions.

Tips for Teachers

- *Teach a process.* Teach the ways of collecting information—don't just expect students to know how to do it. If you have students working together in groups, decide on one or two processes that they will be using and teach these to the group, such as outlining. You might add another process every few days. You can place students in different groups according to what process you plan on teaching. Some students may already know a process, whereas others need to learn it or be refreshed on how to use it.

- *Bookmark Web sites.* Visit Web sites before you have the students use them. Make a list of professional sites that will contain unbiased and more reliable information. You might want to bookmark these for quick reference. Much time can be wasted by having students surf the Web to find information.

- *Identify school resources.* Use the resources inside of your school or classroom for preliminary research before looking for other resources. This will help identify the types of information and other resources that are still needed to answer the questions.

What is the best way for students to develop a product to share?

- *Decide on a product*—Review a variety of products to understand possible options.
- *Organize a product plan*—List the steps that will be followed to develop the product.
- *Create the product*—Spend ample time, thought, and creativity to design and make the product.

Chapter 7 Overview

Chapter 7
Developing a Product

It is the supreme art of the teacher to awaken joy in creative expression and knowledge.
—A. Einstein

About Developing a Product

Our small group of third-grade gifted students had spent several weeks collecting information about a variety of topics. They were ready to develop products to share with their peers and parents. We sat in a circle as we asked the students to think about their questions. One teacher said, "I'm going to describe a possible product that you might be interested in developing. I want you to think if you will be able to share the information about your questions using that product." As she described each of the Developing a Product Resource Cards and passed them around the circle, Alan's face lit up when he saw the diagram. One of his questions related to the characteristics of a bee. He knew that the diagram would be a perfect match. He smiled and quietly ignored the remaining products that were shared. The teacher reminded the group, "Now, look at each of your questions and make sure that your product will provide enough information to answer *all* of your questions." Suddenly Alan, looking stunned, realized that the diagram would answer only one of his questions! Because he had conducted an experimental study with bees in his backyard, we guided him in selecting graphs and a journal summary as two additional products. Now, he relaxed. He was ready to begin creating his products.

In this lesson, we nurture students' thinking about deciding on a product that most effectively communicates the information they have learned and answers the study questions. We turn attention to four aspects of developing a product: (a) understanding the purpose of creating a product, (b) matching a product to best represent students' learning about a topic and assuring that it is appropriate for the audience, (c) making a product plan of sequenced steps and estimated time, and (d) developing the product. Constructing the products may be the most enjoyable part of the independent study for many students. This is where their creativity emerges as they find interesting ways to present their information to others.

Objective

1. The students will select and develop a product that answers the study questions about his or her topic and matches his or her audience.

Key Concepts

- *Product*—Something that is created or performed to give information to others.
- *Product plan*—An organized way that is worked out in advance to show how the product will be developed.

Materials for Teaching

- Resource Cards 73–103
- Examples of student products from previous years
- Student Booklets (pp. 37–40)

Evaluation Questions

1. Did the students select and develop products that answered the questions about their topics?
2. Did the students select and develop products that matched the age and interests of the audience?

Developing a Product

Lesson 1: The Purpose of Products

1. Discuss with students, "Now, that you have studied a topic and have found answers to the study questions you asked about that topic, how will you share your information with an audience?" (They may give a variety of answers, such as "tell them" or "show them something.") If you have brought in sample products from past independent studies, they may refer to them. Indicate how each of the products answered the study questions and matched the interest and age level of the audience.

2. Explain that the main purpose of developing a product is to share information they have learned about their topic with an audience in the most effective way. The product that they develop should answer the study questions. There are many possible products that they might develop.

3. Have students open their Student Booklets to Chapter 7: Developing a Product (see p. 37). Read the definition of *product*. "A product is something that is created or performed to give information to others about the questions you have studied."

4. Have students think about what information from their questions they will need to present (e.g., characteristics of bees, their feeding habits). Have them summarize briefly in their Student Booklets the information that they learned about their questions. Have them share some of this information with the rest of the group. Write this information on the board.

5. If an audience has not already been selected, have them identify an audience who might be interested in their information. They will want to think about products the audience might enjoy and that also will present the answers to their study questions. Have the students describe the audience on p. 37 in their Student Booklet. Write this information on the board.

6. Tell the students about possible product options by sharing the Resource Card examples (see Resource Cards 73–103). First, describe a product from one of the Resource Cards. Look at the list on the board and ask, "Would this product share this information? Would it be interesting to this audience?" Guide the students in deciding if the product matches the information and the audience. Go through several of the Resource Cards in this way, listing a variety of products and discussing their relationship to each of the information items and audiences.

7. Share products, pictures of products, and stories about products that other students have developed, if possible. Make the connection of how each product answered specific questions from their study.

    Below is a story that you might want to share with your students.

    Tyrone asked these questions: "What are the characteristics of dolphins?", "How was the dolphin chosen as the school's mascot?", and "Is the dolphin a good school mascot?" Tyrone researched his topic by highlighting and taking notes from the Internet and books. He interviewed teachers who were teaching in the school during the time the dolphin was selected as the mascot. He also created a survey and administered it to the students in his school. Tyrone decided that he wanted to share his information about dolphins and the results from his survey and interviews on a presentation board. On the board, he placed
    1. facts about the characteristics of dolphins using dolphin foldouts (the question was on the outside of the dolphin and the answer was on the inside),
    2. graphs that showed the answers to the questions from the student surveys,
    3. a summary of the answers to the interview questions about the history of selecting the mascot, and
    4. pictures of dolphins.

    Because Tyrone knew that he was going to be presenting his information to first-grade students, he also planned a short puppet show that reenacted the student survey that he had administered to his classmates. In this way, the young children would learn about the answers to his questions in a fun way that would be appealing to them.

Developing a Product 115

8. Have the students summarize how Tyrone's product choices matched the audience and his questions. Have the students write in their Student Booklets (see p. 37) some possible products that they might develop to showcase their information.

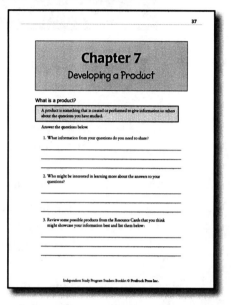

Lesson 2: Selecting the Best Products

1. Say, "Choosing the best product is no easy feat! In this lesson, you are going to be learning how to select the best product for your study." Have students consider who the audience will be in order to ensure that their product is a good match for the group. Discuss the following questions:
   - Who is the audience? How many people?
   - What is the age of the audience?
   - What visuals might be used to interest the audience?
   - What performances might be used to interest the audience?
   - Which products might be easily seen and understood by the audience?
   - What product might showcase the information learned most effectively?

2. In their Student Booklets, students can select and evaluate several products. Guide them to think about evaluation criteria that they might want to use (remind them to consider the information that they have gathered about all of their questions and the audience). Which product:
   - gives the audience the *most* information about my study questions?
   - is the *most* appealing to this audience?
   - answers the study questions *best*?
   - is the *most* interesting to me to develop?
   - is *easiest* to develop within the timeframe?
   - has the *most* resources available to develop the product?
   - *best* showcases my knowledge and technical skills?

   Have the students decide on five products and place them on the rows of the product evaluation matrix in the Student Booklet (see p. 38). Have them list three criteria and write them in the columns.

3. Have students look at one criterion at a time. They should ask themselves the question and put a "5" (or the number of topics being judged) in the box next to the topic that best fits the criterion. They should put a "1" next to the topic that fits the criterion the least. A "4" is placed by the next best, a "2" for the next least, and a "3" for the one that is

Developing a Product

left over. When they have judged each topic against each criterion, they will add the numbers next to each solution and put the sum in the Total box. The highest total becomes the best product to develop. Note that the student may need to develop several products, similar to Tyrone, to provide information about all of his or her questions.

4. Conclude this lesson by asking, "What have you learned about selecting a product? Describe the process that you used in identifying a product. What resources and methods helped you the most? The least? What would you do the same or differently the next time?"

Lesson 3: Making a Product Plan

1. Tell the students that once they have decided on the specific product(s) to create, they will need a plan to guide them through its (their) development.

2. Share Resource Cards 73–103 with the students. Say, "The Resource Cards provide steps for developing these products: book, diagram, diorama, game, graph, poster, PowerPoint presentation, puppet show, report, tape recording, television show, timeline, videotape or DVD, and Web page." Let the students review the Resource Cards for their selected products individually, in pairs, or in small groups.

3. To help the students elaborate the specific characteristics of their product, guide the students through a visualization of their products by saying (remember to pause for a few seconds after each question to allow the students to paint a picture in their minds): "Hmmm. I want to present my information with this product or these products. . . . What will it look like? . . . What colors will I use? . . . What materials will I use? . . . Do I want the audience to touch it? . . . What size will it be? . . . Will it be very large? . . . Very small? . . . What parts will it have? . . . Will there be moving parts? . . . Will I move it? . . . Will I draw it? . . . Will I construct it? . . . Will I use photos? . . . Will I use a computer to help me show it? . . . Will I use words or a story to tell about it? . . . Will I have the audience listen to it? . . . Will I have the audience do something with it? . . . Will I show them how to do something? . . . Now, in your Student Booklet (see p. 39), sketch a visual representation of the product you were thinking about."

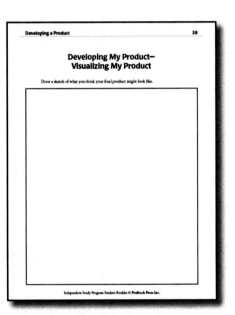

4. As the students are sketching their products, you will sketch a picture of a possible product such as an owl book on the board for later discussion. Share your sketch and then have the students share their sketches with one another.

Developing a Product

5. Have students turn to Making My Product Plan in their Student Booklets (see p. 40) and read the definition aloud, "A product plan is a guide used in planning and developing the product."

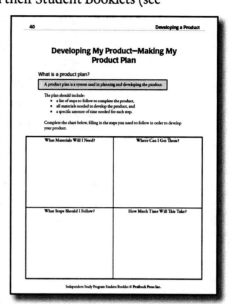

6. Have students think through the steps needed for their products or use the ones presented on the Resource Cards. Have them write these steps in the Student Booklet. Model your thinking of how you might do this:

> I need to think how I want to present my information in my owl-shaped book. I may need to go to a picture book to see exactly how an author puts a picture book together. (Hold up a picture book and think aloud how you notice specific details.) I will have a book cover, inside the book cover I'll have 'All About the Author'—that's me. Then a title page—what do you notice here? The following pages have text on both sides of the page and pictures. There's a blank page at the back and then the back cover. Well, that's a start. My book is nonfiction with lots of information about owls, so I may peruse some nonfiction books to see how they organize their subtopics.
>
> In my Student Booklet, let me jot down what steps I will follow. (Have this prepared ahead of time and put on the overhead so they can see the steps.)
>
> 1. Type the text. (3 class periods)
> 2. Draw the pictures on each page. (2 periods)
> 3. Write the "About the Author" for inside cover. (1 period)
> 4. Make the title page. (½ period)
> 5. Cut out the owl-shaped book covers and decorate. (1 period)
> 6. Bind the book. (½ period)
>
> Materials needed: paper bag or brown construction paper for the owl-shaped cover, crayons for the drawings, twine and a hole punch for the binding, white paper for inside pages

7. Now, tell students to think about their product plan, visualizing it, just like you did when you presented the think-aloud. Give them time to write their estimations in the Student Booklet. Reassure them that this is only an estimate of the time they think it might take. It may take more or less time than they anticipate. They can write the actual time beside each step as they go through them. This process will help them better gauge their time on the next product they develop.

8. Summarize the lesson by having the students share the products that they will develop and some of the materials and steps that they will use in developing it.

Lesson 4: Developing the Product

1. Have students bring the materials they need from home or help them locate materials at school or from local businesses.

2. For the next few days or class periods, allow students time to work on their products in class. Students who have similar products may work together. Encourage a helping attitude so that the class works cooperatively to support each other. Peer helpers and parent volunteers who have special skills may be used.

3. Your role as the teacher will be to supply resources and to help guide individuals and small groups of students in developing their products. You may use the Resource Cards to provide information about specific steps, the Internet to find more products and/or more steps that will help in designing products not listed on the Resource Cards, and previous student products or volunteers to show specific techniques for making products.

Ideas for Primary Students

- Show one or two possible products and teach students step-by-step how to develop them. Give students a limited choice so that you can walk them through the process together. You are helping to build their skills so that they will be better prepared in upper grades to complete increasingly sophisticated products.

Tips for Teachers

- *Photographs.* Take photographs of the products this group of students develops so that you have examples to show the next class.

- *Limit the products.* Decide if you want all students to develop the same product, such as a PowerPoint presentation or a tri-fold display, and teach the step-by-step process to the entire class. Or, you might teach several different products to small groups. For a first independent study, limiting the number of products allows you more control to assist as needed.

- *Allow class time.* You may want to allow time during class for students to develop products in school. (This way, you are assured that it is totally the students' work.) It also allows the teacher to guide the studies and to help students learn the process as they gain independence. If some products will take longer than others to complete, students may need to finish parts at home.

Chapter 8 Overview

What is the best way for students to present information?

- *Oral report*—A verbal telling of information to others.
- *Demonstration*—A physical display that shows how something is done.
- *Performance*—An action that conveys information in an artistic manner.
- *Display*—A visual collection of information that presents it in an organized and interesting way.
- *Electronic display*—A visual showing of information on a computer or other electronic device.
- *Combination*—Most reports will combine a verbal and visual presentation.

Chapter 8
Presenting Information

That which we persist in doing becomes easier, not that the task itself has become easier, but that our ability to perform it has improved.
—Ralph Waldo Emerson

About Presenting Information

Presentations are important to children. They provide students with an opportunity to present the information to a real audience—information they have spent much time thinking about, and much effort preparing. The importance that students placed on this part of independent studies became evident to me when I was consulting in Kathy Robertson's fifth-grade class as students were digging deeply into mythology. I went into her class every week for a month, working with individual students to guide, assist, and support their thinking. Sometimes I met with small groups that were collecting information in a similar way or a pair of children who were developing related presentations.

When presentation week rolled around, I walked into the room and was astounded. Many boys were dressed in coats and ties; some girls were in dresses with ribbons in their hair. They were all sitting quietly, eager expressions on their faces, big smiles hiding words that were ready to burst out to share their information. They were prepared. They were ready to share with their classmates and with me what they had studied so long and hard all month. They were independent learners—and proud!

This lesson actively engages students in preparing and showcasing their learning in several ways. It covers clear directions about how to give an effective presentation and guides students to practice, evaluate, and revise before making the final presentation. We hope to lift students' levels of performance by guiding them to hold high standards for themselves as they constantly strive to improve.

Objective

The students will present their independent study to an audience.

Key Concepts

- *Oral report*—Sharing information with others in spoken form.
- *Demonstration*—A physical display that shows how something is done.
- *Performance*—An action that conveys information in an artistic manner.
- *Display*—A collection of information arranged for others to see in a visually appealing, interesting, or entertaining way.
- *Electronic display*—Information and graphics that are shown on a computer monitor or on another electronic device.

Materials for Teaching

- Resource Cards 104–111
- Student Booklets (pp. 41–42)
- Examples of various ways of presenting information

Evaluation Questions

1. Did the students select and develop a way of presenting their information to an audience?
2. Did the students present their information to an audience?
3. Did the students evaluate their information using themselves, their peers, and/or the audience?

Lesson 1: The Purpose and Types of Presentations

1. Write the word *presentations* on the board and place a K-W-L chart underneath (K = what I **K**now; W = what I **W**ant to know; L = what I've **L**earned). Ask students if they have ever presented information to others. Ask, "Who was the audience? What did you do? Why did you present your information?" Ask them what they previously learned (and now know) about making presentations. List their ideas on the board under the "K." Ask them what they would like to learn about making presentations. Place these ideas under the "W" on the board. Tell them that in this lesson they are going to learn more about making presentations and ways to present their independent studies.

2. Have the students open their Student Booklets to Chapter 8: Presenting Information (see p. 41). Discuss with the students the reasons and importance of presenting the information they have studied. Ask, "What might others learn about your study? How might you get ideas from other people? How might you improve your product after the presentation? Why would you need to gain support from other people? How might others evaluate your study?"

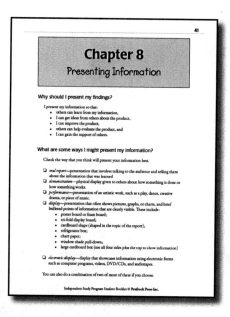

3. Write the following ways of presenting information on the board: *oral reports, demonstrations, performances, displays, electronic displays* and *combination*. Have the students follow along in their Student Booklets as you briefly describe each of these ways and have them give you an example of each. Place the students' examples from the discussion beside each of the different ways.

    - *Oral reports.* Oral reports are presentations that involve talking to the audience members and telling them about the information that was learned.
    - *Demonstrations.* A demonstration is a display given to others of how something is done or how something works. It might be a reenactment of an experiment or a slow motion demonstration showing the steps of

a skill, such as how to hit a one-handed backhand in tennis, or how to plan a new game.
- *Performances*. Performances are presentations of an artistic work, such as a play, a dance, a creative drama, or playing a piece of music.
- *Displays*. Displays can give the audience information visually. They often show pictures, graphs or charts, and brief bulleted points of information that are clearly visible. The most effective ones use colorful, big, bold text to highlight sections.
- *Electronic displays*. Electronic displays showcase information using electronic forms such as computer programs, videos, and DVD/CDs.

4. After you have briefly described each of the ways of presenting information, tell the students that you are going to show them what an oral report looks and sounds like. You will want them to pay close attention to what you do when introducing your study. Below is an example of the beginning of a report on wolves.

Wolves—Friends or Enemies?

(*Play the sound of a wolf howling—something that can be found in a public library or online.*) Tell the students,

> That was the sound of a wolf in the wild. Most of us have never heard that sound in real life, but what picture does it create in your mind? When you think of wolves, do you think of scary stories you've read about the Big Bad Wolf and werewolves or do you think of beautiful dog-like animals that look like German Shepherds? (Hold up two pictures, one that is a scary storybook wolf and one that is a beautiful dog-like photograph.) Today, I'm going to share with you some information I learned about wolves.

5. Discuss what was effective about the way you presented your introduction. (Students should notice that you grabbed their attention with a sound, made a personal connection with something they all knew about such as wolves, gave them a forced choice to nudge their thinking, showed pictures to create interest, and asked a question.) They don't need to include all of these strategies in their introduction and report, but let them think about and focus on a few interesting ways to get information across to their audience.

Presenting Information   **129**

Ways to Make an Effective Oral Report

Before:
- ✔ Arrange the materials in order.
- ✔ Rehearse it for someone.
- ✔ Get feedback and use it.

During:
- ✔ Introduce yourself, if necessary.
- ✔ Begin with an interesting hook to draw the audience in (e.g., an interesting question or story).
- ✔ Use visual or sound props.
- ✔ Hold props so everyone can see.
- ✔ State clear points about a few subtopics.
- ✔ Talk to the audience, don't just read the report.
- ✔ Repeat the few major points at the end.

After:
- ✔ Ask if anyone has questions or comments.
- ✔ Have the audience evaluate the presentation.
- ✔ Thank them for listening.

Figure 9. Ways to make an effective report.

6. Make a chart entitled "Ways to Make an Effective Oral Report" and list their ideas. See Figure 9 for an example.

7. At the conclusion of this discussion, ask the students if they have identified some possible ways that they might like to present their information and list their names next to each of the ways. Ask the students what they have learned, and place their responses in the "L" column of the K-W-L chart you began filling out at the beginning of class.

Lesson 2: Selecting One or More Ways of Presenting Information

1. Tell the students that they will be learning about the specific steps needed to make their presentations using one or more of the ways discussed in the previous lesson. Using the information from the previous lesson, form groups around specific ways of presenting information, pass out the corresponding Resource Cards, and provide the groups with the examples listed below.
    - *Demonstration.* Have a video, CD, or DVD of someone demonstrating how to do something (e.g., a video or CD from previous presentations or a show from one of the home, cooking, or golf channels might work).
    - *Performance.* You might model a performance using puppets or have a CD or DVD of a performance.
    - *Display.* Have photos or actual examples of previous student displays. Try to show the array of materials that might be used such as poster board or foam board, tri-fold display board, cardboard shape (shaped in the topic of the report), refrigerator box, chart paper, window shade pull-down, and large cardboard box (use all four sides plus the top to show information).
    - *Electronic displays.* Have a handout that shows the various types of electronic media that might be used. Show students some examples of presentations on computer programs, videotape, DVD, or CD as models so that they will have a basis for choosing the appropriate way to showcase their material. See Figure 10 for an example.

2. Have the students look at Resource Cards 104–111 and the examples and notice the characteristics of presenting information.

3. Have the students share the important characteristics with the whole group about presenting information in different ways. Ask, "What have you learned about making presentations?" Add this information to the K-W-L chart under "L." Have each of the students identify the way or ways that he or she will present his or her information.

Presenting Information

Electronic Medium	Examples of Hardware/Software	What It Can Do
Computer program	PowerPoint QuickTime Keynote Kidspiration	Show text, slides, and movies on a computer screen
Video	Digital, Hi-8 mm & VHS formats Video Camera Computer or TV monitor	Capture video clips to document learning projects
Photography	Camera – digital, 35mm, Polaroid, or disposables	Enhance projects with photographs for displays or to insert into digital displays
DVD/CD	DVD/CD burner to record DVD/CD discs TV & DVD/CD player or computer (with DVD/CD player) for playback	Media to store and combine picture, video, and sound
Audiotape	Tape recorder Audio tape	Tape interviews Produce a radio broadcast with sound effects

Figure 10. Examples of electronic media.

Lesson 3: Developing the Presentation

1. Have students bring the materials they need from home or help them locate materials at school or from local businesses.

2. During one or two class periods, allow students time to work on their presentations in class (e.g., making note cards for oral reports, gathering materials for displays, arranging materials on display boards, writing scripts for performances).

3. Your role as the teacher will be to supply resources and to help guide individuals and small groups of students in learning how to present information. You may use the Resource Cards to provide information about specific steps or previous student products to show specific techniques for developing displays. You may want to have small workshops for teaching some of the computer programs that can be used for electronic displays.

Lesson 4: Practicing and Critiquing Presentations

1. When the students have all of their materials ready for the presentation, have the students look at the questions in the Student Booklet on p. 42.

   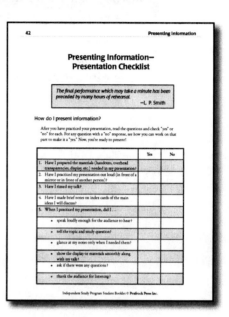

2. Model a "good" and a "poor" presentation for the students. For example, when presenting a book report, talk very softly, don't look at the students, and don't show them the book. Have them critique your presentation. Emphasize the importance of providing positive feedback and the ways of providing positive feedback—using "I statements" and words that describe the behavior (e.g., I like the way that you showed your material; I thought that you talked loudly enough for everyone to hear; I liked the way you organized your information; I liked how you maintained eye contact and smiled).

3. Have the students use paired learning to practice their presentations. Review paired learning using Resource Card 6.

   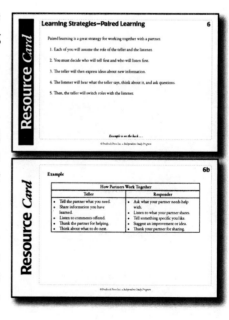

4. Using the Student Booklet, have each of the students self-evaluate his or her practiced presentation with the checklist before presenting. It will help the students identify what they did well, as well as a few places that need more practice or attention.

5. Have the students develop a form that the audience will use in evaluating their presentations. The student might want to use some of the questions in his or her Student Booklet, as well as some questions specific to his or her own topic.

Ideas for Primary Students

- Teach students one or two ways to present their information, so they are not overwhelmed with possibilities. As students do more independent studies, they can add to their repertoire. Most important, model the process for them. Demonstrate how a display might look. Show them how you think through the process of putting a display together. Think aloud as you create a display in front of the class using a small amount of information. Keep it brief and simple.

- If students are particularly shy about presenting, you may want to videotape them and use this medium to help them make the presentation. In this way, they will only need to answer the audience's questions—not make an entire oral presentation.

Presenting Information

> ### Tips for Teachers
>
> - *Show Presenting Information early.* Students may need to know about the different types of presentations before they collect all of their information, so that they can prepare their notes most efficiently. The process of independent study is not always a linear one. It can move in and out of each step in a circular and spiraling way. Some students may need to review the Resource Cards 104–111 on Presenting Information earlier in their study.
>
> - *Show examples.* Keep a few examples or photos of quality independent study projects to show next year's students. Over time, you will develop a repertoire of various kinds of presentations. You might make copies of electronic displays or of student-generated books and reports. Although you don't want students to copy exactly what they see, giving them a wide array of ideas can help jump-start their own thinking and encourage them to go beyond the ordinary.
>
> - *Self-evaluate.* Have each student self-evaluate by completing a checklist from the Student Booklet after the presentation. When teachers promote reflections, students develop lifelong skills and take responsibility for their own learning.
>
> - *Audience evaluations.* You may choose to have the audience evaluate each presentation or simply have various students tell what was effective and enjoyable about each presentation. It's meaningful for students to receive encouraging responses from their peers or from their audiences. It's also important for students to practice giving positive feedback to others.

How might the independent study be evaluated?

- *Self*—Students reflect about their experiences: what they did well and what they might have done differently for a more effective study.
- *Teacher*—Teachers evaluate the positive aspects and identify areas that need improving.
- *Audience*—The audience that is presented the information provides support and suggestions.

What are the different types of evaluation tools available?

- *Rubric*—A set of guidelines that identify specific areas of focus.
- *Checklist*—A list of items to guide students.
- *Rating scale*—A way of judging something on a numerical scale.
- *Direct observation*—A way of noticing and recording specific information.

Chapter 9 Overview

Chapter 9
Evaluating the Independent Study

That's what education means, to be able to do what you've never done before.
—A. F. Palmer

About Evaluating the Independent Study

Austin, a fourth grader, was interested in volcanoes, particularly Mount St. Helens, because his grandmother had lived near the volcano when it erupted. He became immersed in his study, gathering information about volcanoes from books, the Internet, and interviews with his grandmother and her friends in Washington. When it came time for his presentation, he decided not only to write a small booklet about volcanoes but also to engage his first-grade audience by building a model and demonstrating a volcanic eruption, using a little vinegar, baking soda, dish detergent, and food coloring. Indeed, during the presentations, the young children wanted to see his volcano "erupt" over and over again. Austin eventually allowed his young audience to join him in the demonstration. When he evaluated his study with his teacher, he quickly rated himself highly in all areas—still excited about the attention he received from the audience. In fact, one strength of his study was his "consideration of the audience when he made the presentation." However, as he started to review more carefully each of the criteria, he realized that he didn't address his More Thinking Questions in his product or his presentation—those related to the future of the Cascade range. Although he had enjoyed developing his products and learning many facts about volcanoes, he omitted thinking more deeply about his questions and decided that those would be the focus of his next study.

Evaluation of independent studies involves much more than simply giving a letter grade at the end. It requires careful thinking throughout the learning experience. Assessment points have been included throughout the independent study, which we hope you have used.

In this lesson, we cover three aspects of evaluating students' work through their independent studies: the *process*, the *product*, and the *content*. The process is the way students use strategies through each step of research and their disposition toward learning. The product is the way that students choose to show what they have learned. The content is the topic they are studying. There are several methods of assessing the process, product, and content. It is important to look at how each student has learned and grown through the entire independent study experience.

In addition to the way we evaluate, we also need to consider who should evaluate students' research: the students, the teacher, and the actual audience to which the information is presented. In this way, students receive the important feedback they deserve in ways that will help them think deeply about their learning and know how to improve on the next independent study they undertake.

Objective

The students will evaluate their learning at the conclusion of the independent study.

Key Concepts

- *Evaluation*—Examining the completed work and analyzing the strengths and weaknesses of the study.
- *Rubric*—A set of guidelines that identify specific areas of focus.
- *Checklists*—A list of items to guide students.
- *Rating scales*—A way of judging something on a numerical scale.
- *Direct observation*—A way of noticing and recording specific information.

Materials for Teaching

- Resource Card 112
- Student Booklets (pp. 43–46)

Evaluation Questions

1. Did the students evaluate the content of their independent studies?
2. Did the students evaluate the process of their independent studies?
3. Did the students evaluate the product of their independent studies?
4. Were they able to analyze their strengths and weaknesses?
5. Were they able to identify areas for improvement?

Evaluating the Independent Study

Lesson 1: Why do you evaluate?

1. Write the word *evaluation* on the board with its definition: "Examining the work that has been done during the independent study and analyzing the strengths and weaknesses of the study."

2. Discuss with the students why it is important for them to evaluate their independent studies.

3. List these reasons on the board and then star the reasons that the students feel are most important. Emphasize the opportunity for improvement rather than grades.

4. Have the students turn to Chapter 9: Evaluating My Independent Study in their Student Booklet (see p. 43). Explain each item of the evaluation (e.g., what it means "to use time efficiently"). Have students give both positive and negative examples of each criterion.

5. Summarize by providing verbal or visual examples from previous studies to see if the students are able to evaluate them using the criteria.

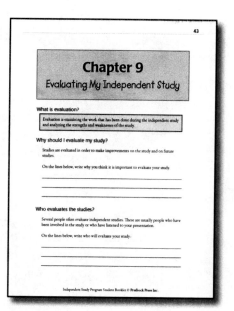

Lesson 2: Using the Evaluation Tools

1. Direct the students to complete the self-evaluation forms after their presentations using the one in the Student Booklet (see p. 44) or those in Appendix C. You should also fill out an evaluation for each student.

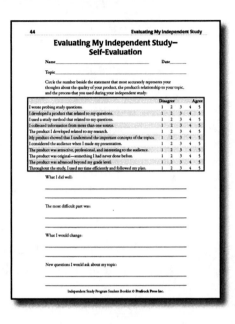

2. Meet with students individually to compare their evaluations with yours. When comparing and talking about the evaluations, remember these important points:
    - begin with the positive aspects of the study,
    - attend to what the student has learned,
    - focus on the process rather than just the product,
    - identify areas to improve in the next independent study,
    - discuss new questions that may have arisen in working on this independent study, and
    - ask what the student might still wonder or have questions about his or her topic.

3. Discuss with the students ideas for future studies based on what they have learned and further questions he or she might have about that topic.

4. Celebrate the students' learning and their studies at the end of the process. You might want to consider further presentations such as:
    - a presentation day for parents to showcase their efforts;
    - a museum display in the room, hall, or library for the entire school to observe;
    - a class newsletter in which students write blurb summaries about their studies; and
    - a presentation to a community group or the city council about a current issue.

Evaluating the Independent Study

5. You also may want to consider taking digital photographs of the students with their products to post on the school Web site or display on the hall bulletin board. This will provide examples for next year's students.

> **Ideas for Primary Students**
>
> - Select the primary version of the Evaluation Form so that they focus on a few important aspects. Grades are certainly secondary to the importance of their learning and thinking through what they did well and what they want to do better next time.

Evaluating the Independent Study

Tips for Teachers

- *Review evaluation at the beginning.* Tell students before they begin their independent studies how they are going to be assessed and evaluated during each step and at the end. In this way, they will have a guide for learning and be able to observe and improve the process of their studies.

- *Select evaluation tool.* Select a checklist, rubric, rating scale, and direct observation to assess and evaluate the independent study project. They each have their own special features and value. Decide which best fits your purposes and needs. Samples are included in Appendix C for you to copy for each student or use as models to create your own.

- *Focus on learning.* Remember that the point of the evaluation is to improve the student's ability to conduct research independently. Don't make grades the overall focus—the student may become more interested in the grade than the learning, and that is not what is important.

- *Teach how to evaluate.* For the most part, students tend to evaluate themselves more harshly than you will. In these cases, it is easy to point out examples of their strengths and have them see how well they did. If you have students who overrate themselves, you may want to consider using the evaluation as a teachable moment to help them see how to evaluate. For example, you might say, "It appears that you and I have some disagreement about the evaluations. Let me show you how I determined my rating." Then show them examples from the Student Booklet, student conferences, and so on. Tell them that you looked for how often a behavior occurred and its quality. If the student appears to understand how you evaluated his or her strengths and weaknesses, you might stop the evaluation and say, "I know that because you now understand the process better, you will do a better job next time." On the other hand, if the student provides explanations for his or her ratings that are logical, you might say, "You and I need to meet more frequently so that I am aware of all that you are doing. Thank you for giving me this good information."

Appendix A
Teacher Resources

Using the Scope of Independent Study Skills

This scope of independent study skills addresses the concepts outlined in the nine chapters. The skills are clustered by step and arranged linearly from selecting a topic to evaluation. The sequence of steps does not preclude the knowledgeable teacher's rearrangement. In fact, this rearrangement is encouraged in adapting instruction to individual differences and enhancing the circular process of independent study. For example, we have found that some teachers teach note taking and outlining before beginning the program; others omit the Organizing a Topic and Using a Study Method sections, teaching only the descriptive method and collecting factual information until the students have mastered skills in the other sections; others teach only one or two of the skills in each area, increasing the number as the students become more proficient.

You will want to identify which skills will be taught to your class during the first independent study. As you discover the students' background knowledge, you may want to modify this skills list. Remember to select a small number of skills for the first study so that students are able to understand the whole process in a short period of time.

For example, you might select a topic for the students to study. With the students, have them ask one or two "W" questions and collect factual information through interviews and several books. You might then teach them to develop PowerPoint presentations and share these products during the school open house. The teacher, individual students, and the audience at the open house could then evaluate the studies.

In this example, you made some of the decisions and limited choices. For the next independent study, you might expand the number skills needed by allowing students to select topics, develop higher levels of questions, adding additional methods for gathering information, and including more product choices.

You might also want to use the scope of independent study skills to create a class growth chart (see a model form on p. 150 following the Scope of Independent Study Skills). In this case, you would indicate on this form the skills that the students know, those that they learn, and those that they will need to learn.

These types of forms become helpful in following students' progress and developing their skills across grade levels. As a team of teachers, you might decide which skills you will teach primary, intermediate, middle school, and high school students.

Appendix A: Teacher Resources

Scope of Independent Study Skills

I. **Introduction**
   A. Define and describe the steps of independent study
   B. Tell what a topic is
   C. Develop a plan for an independent study

II. **Selecting a Topic**
   A. Define topics or subtopics
   B. Gather information about a topic
   C. Select one topic using an evaluation procedure
   D. Identify criteria for selecting a topic
   E. Rate topics according to criteria

III. **Organizing a Topic**
   A. Organize a topic using descriptions
   B. Organize a topic using comparisons
   C. Organize a topic using causes and effects
   D. Organize a topic using problems and solutions

IV. **Asking Questions**
   A. Identify effective study questions
   B. Write an effective study question:
      1. using the "W" and "H" words
      2. that requires little thinking
      3. that requires more and most thinking
   C. Select questions to study using an evaluation procedure
   D. Organize questions into a sequence for study

V. **Using a Study Method**
   A. Use the factual study method—collect facts about something.
   B. Use the descriptive study method—describe a topic with numbers and facts
   C. Use the historical study method—examine the past or history of a topic
   D. Use the case study method—observe a person, group, or something closely
   E. Use the correlation study method—compare one thing with another using numbers

F. Use the action study method—examine an improvement made to a problem
G. Use the experimental study—conduct an experiment (or quasi-experiment) and collect factual information

VI. Collecting Information
    A. Use different sources that provide information
        1. People
        2. Places
        3. Internet
        4. Electronic sources
        5. Objects/materials for experiments
        6. Print/text
    B. Use different methods for collecting information from the sources.
        1. Conducting experiments
        2. Corresponding (writing e-mails or letters)
        3. Interviewing
        4. Observing
        5. Reading
        6. Searching the Internet
        7. Surveying
    C. Organize information that has been collected
        1. Classifying
        2. Outlining
        3. Summarizing
        4. Taking notes
        5. Using index cards
        6. Webbing

VII. Developing a Product
    A. Select a product that matches the questions and the audience
    B. Plan the development of a product
    C. Create a product
        1. Book
        2. Diagram
        3. Diorama
        4. Game
        5. Graph
        6. Poster
        7. PowerPoint slideshow

Appendix A: Teacher Resources

       8. Puppet show
       9. Report
     10. Tape recording
     11. Television show
     12. Timeline
     13. Video
     14. Web page

VIII. Presenting Information
    A. Use an oral report to present information
    B. Prepare a demonstration to present information
    C. Prepare a performance to present information
    D. Prepare a display to present information
    E. Prepare an electronic display to present information

IX. Evaluating the Study
    A. Self-evaluate
    B. Identify strengths
    C. Focus on what to improve for the next study
    D. Compare self-evaluation with teacher and audience evaluations

Class Growth Chart Example

Names of Students	Independent Study Skills									
	1C	2C	3A	4B	5A	6A	6B3	6C1	7C7	8A	9
1.											
2.											
3.											
4.											
5.											
6.											
7.											
8.											
9.											
10.											
11.											
12.											
13.											
14.											
15.											
16.											
17.											
18.											
19.											
20.											

Conference Planning Guide

Name _____ Date _____

Independent Study Topic _____

Circle type of conference: Selecting a Topic

                                    Organizing a Topic

                                    Asking Questions

                                    Using a Study Method

                                    Collecting Information

                                    Developing a Product

                                    Presenting Information

                                    Evaluating the Study

During the conference, I want to focus on:

_____

_____

_____

_____

_____

_____

_____

_____

Student Interest Inventory

Name _____ Date _____

1. What is your favorite subject at school? Reading? Music? Social studies? Art? Science? Math? P.E.? Other?

2. What do you like to do when you come home from school?

3. Do you collect anything? If so, what do you collect?

4. Do you like to read? What are your favorite books?

5. If you had to select a nonfiction book to read today, what subjects would interest you?

6. What do you feel that you are good at?

7. Where have you taken any special vacations?

Student Interest Inventory

8. Are there any places you would like to visit?

9. Who are some well-known people that you are curious about?

10. What are your favorite movies? Songs? Type of music? TV shows?

11. What do you like to do with your family?

12. What do you like to do with your friends?

13. What would you like to be when you grow up?

14. Is there anything you would like to know more about?

Sample Note to Parents

Dear Parents,

Your children are beginning an exciting research project that allows them to learn about something they are interested in. This might be part of a unit of study in the classroom or a topic they have chosen on their own. Some children have done this kind of research before, but for others, this is a first-time adventure.

This kind of independent study allows students to think deeply about a topic and to research information in an organized and structured way that helps to nurture their thinking. They will learn to ask questions, organize their topics, search for information from many resources, and share their findings with their classmates and possibly other audiences.

Although this is an independent learning process, the teacher will be involved along the way to guide and encourage students as they enjoy becoming lifelong learners.

Please support your children in their quest for knowledge by asking questions and having them tell you interesting information they have found through their studies.

Appendix B
Student Resources

SCAMPER

S **Substitute**
Who or what else instead? Other ingredient, material, place?

C **Combine**
Put several things together; blend.

A **Adapt or Add**
What else is it like? How could it be changed?

M **Modify, Magnify, or Minimize**
Change the meaning, add to it, or give it a new twist; make it bigger, longer, or taller; make it smaller, shorter, or narrower.

P **Put to Other Uses**
Use in other places; use in a new way.

E **Eliminate**
Take something away; make it smaller, lower, or shorter.

R **Rearrange or Reverse**
Make another pattern or different sequence. What is the opposite? Can you turn it around?

Note-Taking Example

I. History
    A. Early commercial uses
        1. Revenue marine
        2. Privateers
        3. Slavery
    B. Early sporting uses
        1. World's Fair of 1851
        2. New York Yacht Club

II. Current yachts
    A. Daysailers
        1. Characteristics
        2. Use
    B. Offshore ocean racers
        1. Characteristics
        2. Use

III. Races
    A. "One-design" race
        1. Board specifications
        2. Location
    B. "Handicap" race
        1. Handicap specifications
        2. Location

Letter Example

James de Mesquita
Glendale Elementary
24 Congress Avenue
Glendale, OH 45246

April 5, 2007

Ms. Molly Lee
Green Thumb Nursery
15 Maple Circle
Cincinnati, OH 45246

Dear Ms. Lee:

    I'm working on an independent study project about plants in my fourth-grade class. I would like to visit your nursery and learn about the plants that are natural to Ohio. Please let me know if there might be a time that would be convenient to come visit. I am particularly interested in wildflowers.

    I look forward to hearing from you.

Sincerely,

James de Mesquita

cc. Mr. Masters, Teacher
      Mrs. Sussman, Principal

Appendix C
Assessment Forms

Product Rubric

	0	1	2	3	Score
Content	Content was not related to the questions.	Content was related to questions but did not identify important concepts.	Content was related to questions and identified important concepts.	Content was related to questions and identified important concepts. Concepts were creative and/or interdisciplinary.	
Process	The research process is not evident in the product.	The research process is evident in the product but is not authentic.	The research process is evident and is authentic to the topic being studied.	The research process is evident and is authentic to the topic being studied. Process is creative.	
Communication	The audience is not considered in the design of the product.	The audience's age is considered in the design of the product.	The audience's age and interest are considered in the design of the product.	Not only is the audience's age and interest considered, but the audience also is able to interact with the product.	
Technique	The product is not attractive.	The product is attractive.	The product is attractive and is advanced beyond grade level.	Product is attractive, is advanced beyond grade level and uses professional techniques.	
				Total:	

Product Criteria for _____

Criteria	OK	Good	Excellent
How does my product relate to the questions and my research?			
How did I show that I understand the important concepts about my topic?			
How did I use a research method?			
How did I integrate other topics into my study?			
How did I consider the audience when I made my presentation?			
How did I make a product that was attractive, professional, and interesting to the audience?			
How was the product original—something I had never done before?			
How was it advanced, beyond my grade level—what other students would do?			

Student Checklist of Independent Study Progress

	Student Response	
	Yes	No
Selecting a Topic		
• Did I select a topic using an evaluation method? • Did I select a topic that could be studied with available resources within the specified time frame?	____ ____	____ ____
Organizing a Topic		
• Did I select a way to organize my topic that was relevant? • Did I select a process for organizing my topic? • Did I describe some gaps in my knowledge to formulate questions?	____ ____ ____	____ ____ ____
Asking Questions		
• Did I write an effective question that related to my topic? • Did I group my questions in larger categories? • Did I sequence my questions for study?	____ ____ ____	____ ____ ____
Using a Study Method		
• Did I select a method that matched my questions? • Did I describe steps needed to gather information about my questions?	____ ____	____ ____
Collecting Information		
• Did I use different sources for collecting information? • Did I use different methods for collecting information? • Did I use a method for organizing the information I collected?	____ ____ ____	____ ____ ____
Developing Products		
• Did I select and develop products that answered my questions? • Did I select and develop products that matched the age and interests of my audience?	____ ____	____ ____
Presenting Information		
• Did I select and develop a way of presenting my information? • Did I present my information to an audience? • Did I evaluate my information using myself, peers, and/or the audience?	____ ____ ____	____ ____ ____
Evaluating the Study		
• Did I evaluate the content of my independent studies? • Did I evaluate the process of my independent studies? • Did I evaluate the product of my independent studies? • Did I analyze the strengths and weaknesses of my study? • Did I identify how to improve future studies?	____ ____ ____ ____ ____	____ ____ ____ ____ ____

Comments:

Teacher Rating Scale of an Independent Study

Student's Name _____ Date _____

Independent Study Steps	Developing	Competent	Proficient
Selecting a Topic Chooses a topic based on specific criteria			
Organizing a Topic Organizes a topic using one method Identifies gaps to formulate questions			
Asking Questions Writes an effective study question Organizes questions into a sequence			
Using a Study Method Uses a specific method of research			
Collecting Information Uses several sources Uses different methods Organizes information			
Developing a Product Selects product related to questions Develops a product plan Creates a product			
Presenting Information Selects a method for the presentation Presents information to an audience Evaluates presentation			
Evaluating the Study Assesses content, process, and product Analyzes strengths and weaknesses Makes suggestions for improvement			

Independent Study Program Teacher's Guide © Prufrock Press Inc.

Teacher Rating Scale for a Primary Independent Study

Student's Name _____ Date _____

Independent Study Steps	☹	😐	☺
Selecting a Topic Did I select a topic that I liked?			
Asking Questions Did I ask questions about my topic?			
Collecting Information Did I collect information? How?			
Developing a Product Did I develop a product to show what I learned?			
Presenting Information Did I present my study to others?			
Evaluating the Study Did I learn about what I did well and what I needed to learn how to do better?			

Independent Study Program Teacher's Guide © Prufrock Press Inc.

Appendix C: Assessment Forms

Direct Observation—Notes

Student's Name _____

Selecting a Topic:	Date of Observation _____

Organizing a Topic:	Date of Observation _____

Asking Questions:	Date of Observation _____

Using a Study Method (If Applicable):	Date of Observation _____

Collecting Information:	Date of Observation _____

Developing a Product:	Date of Observation _____

Presenting Information:	Date of Observation _____

Evaluating the Study:	Date of Observation _____

Direct Observation—Notes for a Primary Independent Study

Student's Name _____

Selecting a Topic:	Date of Observation _____
Organizing a Topic:	Date of Observation _____
Asking Questions:	Date of Observation _____
Collecting Information:	Date of Observation _____
Developing a Product:	Date of Observation _____
Presenting Information:	Date of Observation _____
Evaluating the Study:	Date of Observation _____

Appendix D
Resource Cards and Student Booklet Thumbnails

Independent Study Program—Index — Card 1

Card Numbers

- How Do I Use the Resource Cards? 2
- Learning Strategies 3–76
- Independent Study Steps
  1. Selecting a Topic 8–9
  2. Organizing a Topic 10–14
  3. Asking Questions 15–19
  4. Using a Study Method 20–38
  5. Collecting Information 39–72
  6. Developing a Product 73–103
  7. Presenting Information 104–111
  8. Evaluating the Study 112

How Do I Use the Resource Cards? — Card 2

The resource cards may be used to:

- Find new ideas.
- Find more information about a specific step.
- Look at examples for understanding something better.
- Learn how to do each independent study step.
- Learn about independent study by yourself.

Learning Strategies — Card 3

- Brainstorming
- SCAMPER
- Paired Learning
- Noticing Special Features

Learning Strategies—Brainstorming — Card 4

How do I brainstorm?

1. Decide on a topic for the group to brainstorm.

2. Follow these rules:
   a. Think of many, varied ideas.
   b. Combine ideas and use everyone's ideas.
   c. Accept all ideas, no matter how wild they may seem at the time.
   d. Avoid judging ideas while they are being given.

3. Allow yourselves plenty of time (at least 10–15 minutes). When you think you have used all of the ideas, add 3–5 more. Often, our best ideas come late!

4. Evaluate the brainstormed list:
   a. Fluency—Did the group think of many ideas (25–50)?
   b. Flexibility—Can ideas be grouped into many different categories?
   c. Originality—Were some ideas unique (you had never heard of them)?
   d. Elaboration—Can you expand or add details to some basic ideas given?

Example is on the back...

Example — Card 4b

Words to use instead of *went* when writing a paragraph:

ran	sashayed	crept
lumbered	pranced	crawled
left	galloped	slipped
strolled	zipped	hobbled
swayed	flew	hopped
shuffled	tottered	skipped
trampled	slithered	frolicked
stomped	sauntered	moved
tip-toed	meandered	traipsed
sallied	staggered	clomped
trudged	bounced	

Learning Strategies—SCAMPER — Card 5

SCAMPER is an acronym (see below) and is a structured form of brainstorming to increase the number of ideas.

- **S** Substitute (Who or what else instead? Other ingredient, material, place, etc.?)
- **C** Combine (Put several things together; blend.)
- **A** Adapt or Add (What else is like it? How could it be changed?)
- **M** Modify, Magnify, or Minimize (Change the meaning, add to it, or give it a new twist; make it bigger, longer, taller; make it smaller, shorter, or narrower.)
- **P** Put to other uses (Use in other places; use in a new way.)
- **E** Eliminate (Take something away; make it smaller, lower, shorter.)
- **R** Rearrange or Reverse (Make another pattern, another sequence. What is the opposite? Turn it around.)

Example is on the back...

Example: How might animals be better managed? — Card 5b

Substitute (put people behind fences instead of animals)

Combine (have communities that must coexist with deer, armadillos, or squirrels)

Adapt (plant foods in the green spaces that wild animals like to eat)

Magnify or Minify (make green spaces larger in the community)

Put to other uses (use golf courses for animal habitats)

Eliminate (guns that would hurt the animals)

Rearrange or Reverse (build communities around the animals' habitats instead of forcing animals into different habitats or into the people's communities)

Learning Strategies—Paired Learning — Card 6

Paired learning is a great strategy for working together with a partner.

1. Each of you will assume the role of the teller and the listener.

2. You must decide who will tell first and who will listen first.

3. The teller will then express ideas about new information.

4. The listener will hear what the teller says, think about it, and ask questions.

5. Then, the teller will switch roles with the listener.

Example is on the back...

Appendix D: Resource Cards and Student Booklet Thumbnails

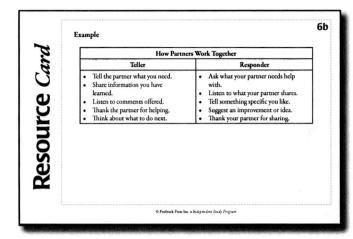

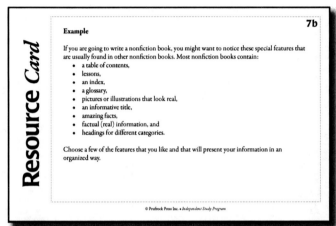

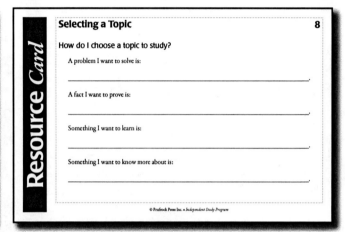

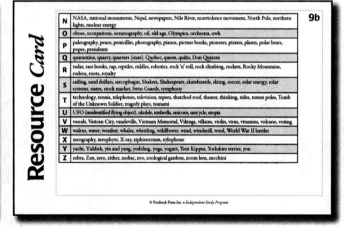

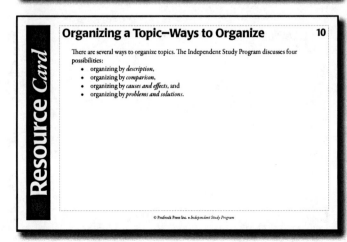

Resource Card 11b

Example: A Way to Organize Your Topic by Description

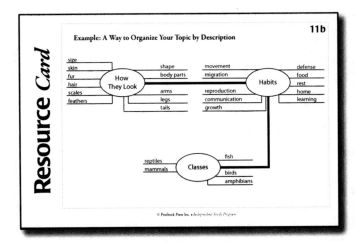

Resource Card 12 — Organizing a Topic—Comparison

1. Tell how your topic's description is the same or how it is different when it is compared to the description of another student's topic, a perfect model, or a rule.

2. Compare your topic with another topic by looking at:
   - how their parts are different or the same,
   - how their history is different or the same,
   - how their growth is different or the same,
   - how people's feelings about them are different or the same,
   - how their uses are different or the same,
   - how their features are different or the same, and
   - how any of your descriptions (from Resource Card 11) are different or the same.

Example is on the back...

Resource Card 12b

Example: A Way to Organize Your Topic by Comparison

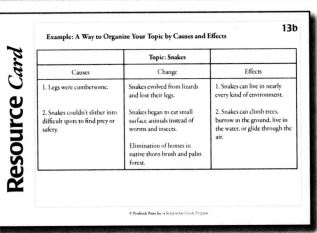

	Animals	
Comparison	Amphibians	Reptiles
1. Appearance	moist skin; lack claws on toes	bony spine; scales or shell
2. Home		
3. Defense		
4. Food		
5. Growth		
6. Communication		

Resource Card 13 — Organizing a Topic—Causes and Effects

1. Identify how the topic has changed or may change. Decide which of the changes you would like to study:
   - changes from the past to the present,
   - changes from the present to the future,
   - changes in its parts or structure,
   - changes in its usefulness,
   - changes in its beliefs or beliefs about it,
   - changes in its purpose, or
   - changes in its habits.

2. Examine the things that always seem to happen before the change (cause) and the things that always seem to happen after the change (effect).

Example is on the back...

Resource Card 13b

Example: A Way to Organize Your Topic by Causes and Effects

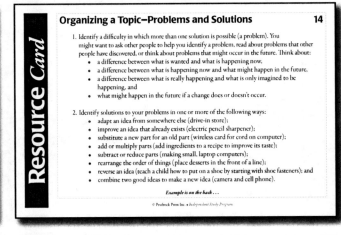

	Topic: Snakes	
Causes	Change	Effects
1. Legs were cumbersome.	Snakes evolved from lizards and lost their legs.	1. Snakes can live in nearly every kind of environment.
2. Snakes couldn't slither into difficult spots to find prey or safety.	Snakes began to eat small surface animals instead of worms and insects. Elimination of homes in native thorn brush and palm forest.	2. Snakes can climb trees, burrow in the ground, live in the water, or glide through the air.

Resource Card 14 — Organizing a Topic—Problems and Solutions

1. Identify a difficulty in which more than one solution is possible (a problem). You might want to ask other people to help you identify a problem, read about problems that other people have discovered, or think about problems that might occur in the future. Think about:
   - a difference between what is wanted and what is happening now,
   - a difference between what is happening now and what might happen in the future,
   - a difference between what is really happening and what is only imagined to be happening, and
   - what might happen in the future if a change does or doesn't occur.

2. Identify solutions to your problems in one or more of the following ways:
   - adapt an idea from somewhere else (drive-in store);
   - improve an idea that already exists (electric pencil sharpener);
   - substitute a new part for an old part (wireless card for cord on computer);
   - add or multiply parts (add ingredients to a recipe to improve its taste);
   - subtract or reduce parts (making small, laptop computers);
   - rearrange the order of things (place desserts in the front of a line);
   - reverse an idea (teach a child how to put on a shoe by starting with shoe fasteners); and
   - combine two good ideas to make a new idea (camera and cell phone).

Example is on the back...

Resource Card 14b

Example: A Way to Organize Your Topic by Problems and Solutions

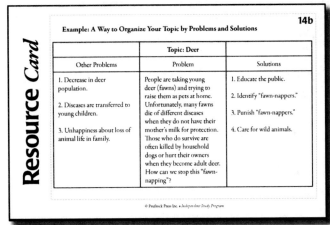

	Topic: Deer	
Other Problems	Problem	Solutions
1. Decrease in deer population.	People are taking young deer (fawns) and trying to raise them as pets at home. Unfortunately, many fawns die of different diseases when they do not have their mother's milk for protection. Those who do survive are often killed by household dogs or hurt their owners when they become adult deer. How can we stop this "fawn-napping"?	1. Educate the public.
2. Diseases are transferred to young children.		2. Identify "fawn-nappers."
3. Unhappiness about loss of animal life in family.		3. Punish "fawn-nappers."
		4. Care for wild animals.

Resource Card 15 — Asking Questions—Good Study Questions

How do I know if I have a good study question?

1. It requires more than one answer.
2. Two people would not give the same answer.
3. I would have time to study it.
4. I would be able to collect information about it.
5. Others might find it useful or beneficial.

Example is on the back...

Appendix D: Resource Cards and Student Booklet Thumbnails

Resource Card 15b — Examples

Poor Study Questions:
- What color is an orange?
- Who invented the telephone?
- How many students are in my class?
- When was Hawaii admitted to the U.S. as a state?

Good Study Questions:
- Why do wars occur?
- How many kinds of insects are in my neighborhood?
- What is the relationship between grades and future achievement?
- Where do new ideas come from?

Note: It is important to remember that a good study question requires more than one answer.

Resource Card 16 — Asking Questions–Using Stem Words

"W" Questions and "H" Questions

There are a number of stem words that can be used to help you write different types of questions. Some words that are often used at the beginning of questions include:
- Who?
- What?
- When?
- Where?
- Why?
- What might happen if?
- How do?
- How many?
- How long?
- How far?

Example is on the back...

Resource Card 16b — Example

Topic: Seals

- Who studies seals?
- What does a seal look like?
- When do seals breed?
- Where do seals live?
- Why are seals protected by treaties?
- What might happen to seals if global warming occurs?
- How do seals communicate?
- How many different types of seals are there?
- How long do seals live?
- How far do seals travel?

Resource Card 17 — Asking Questions–Little Thinking Questions

Questions that require "little thinking" are those that can be answered by simply copying or redoing something that someone else has done. Researchers* who study thinking would consider these types of questions to be those that ask us to *remember* and *understand*.

Little Thinking Questions need to be answered when you are first learning about your topic.

*Anderson, L. W., Krathwohl, D. R., Airasian, P. W., Cruikshank, K. A., Mayer, R. E., Pintrich, P. R., et al. (Eds.). (2001). *A taxonomy for learning, teaching and assessing: A revision of Bloom's taxonomy of educational objectives.* New York: Longman.

Example is on the back...

Resource Card 17b — Examples: Little Thinking Questions

1. What are the different kinds of hummingbirds?

   To answer to this question, you could read a book on birds.

2. What is the story of *Charlotte's Web*?

   To answer to this question, you could read the story and then tell it in your own words.

3. What are the different parts of a computer?

   To answer to this question, you could trace a picture of a computer and label its parts.

Resource Card 18 — Asking Questions–More Thinking Questions

Questions that require "more thinking" are those that can be answered if you use information you already know in new situations. Researchers* would consider these types of questions to be those that ask us to *apply* and *analyze*.

More Thinking Questions may be answered after you know some information about your topic.

*Anderson, L. W., Krathwohl, D. R., Airasian, P. W., Cruikshank, K. A., Mayer, R. E., Pintrich, P. R., et al. (Eds.). (2001). *A taxonomy for learning, teaching and assessing: A revision of Bloom's taxonomy of educational objectives.* New York: Longman.

Example is on the back...

Resource Card 18b — Examples: More Thinking Questions

1. How do you classify birds?

   To answer this question, you could develop a game to teach others how to classify birds.

2. How do gerbils learn?

   To answer this question, you could plan an experiment to show how gerbils might learn.

3. How do students feel about different subjects in school?

   To answer this question, you could have students describe their feelings during each subject and put this information into a chart.

Resource Card 19 — Asking Questions–Most Thinking Questions

Questions that require the "most thinking" are those that can only be answered if you create and/or evaluate new information. Researchers* would consider these types of questions to be those that ask us to *evaluate* and *create*.

Most Thinking Questions are answered by new inventions, creations, or discoveries and require a lot of knowledge about your topic.

*Anderson, L. W., Krathwohl, D. R., Airasian, P. W., Cruikshank, K. A., Mayer, R. E., Pintrich, P. R., et al. (Eds.). (2001). *A taxonomy for learning, teaching and assessing: A revision of Bloom's taxonomy of educational objectives.* New York: Longman.

Example is on the back...

Resource Card 19b

Examples: "Most Thinking" Questions

1. How might I develop a way to protect animals in urban areas?

   To answer this question, you could develop a plan to present to the city council.

2. How do we decide who should be the president of the school's student council?

   To answer this question, you could conduct a survey at your school and develop a set of criteria for this position.

3. How might I teach other students about computers?

   To answer this question, you could develop a set of learning games for the computer and allow students to play them.

Example is on the next Resource Card...

© Prufrock Press Inc. • *Independent Study Program*

Resource Card 20

Using a Study Method—How to Choose

How do I choose a study method?

Look at your study questions and decide on the type of information that you need to collect. You may use more than one study method in your independent study.

Card Numbers

Factual study: Will you need to collect factual information?..........................21–22
Descriptive study: Will you describe something with numbers or facts? 23–24
Historical study: Will you look at the past or history of your topic? 25–26
Developmental study: Will you look at changes or the development of your topic?..... 27–28
Case study: Will you observe a person, group, or something closely? 29–30
Correlation study: Will you compare one thing with another thing using numbers?.....31–32
Action study: Will you look for an improvement? 33–34
Experimental study: Will you set up an experiment and look at the results?...........35–36

© Prufrock Press Inc. • *Independent Study Program*

Resource Card 21

Using a Study Method—Factual Study

How do I collect factual information?

1. Ask a question.
2. Identify resources that you will need to answer the question. If possible, ask other people who may be interested in your topic about good resources.
3. Gather the information from more than one resource.
4. Take notes from the resources.
5. Summarize the information.
6. Identify the information that is factual and the information that is opinion. You will find that factual information is repeated in various resources, whereas opinions may be different in various resources.
   - Fact: Texas is the second largest state in the United States.
   - Opinion: I believe that Texas is the best state to live in.
7. Share the information with others.

Example is on the next Resource Card...

© Prufrock Press Inc. • *Independent Study Program*

Resource Card 22

Using a Study Method—Factual Study Example

Example: How do I collect factual information?

1. Question: What are the characteristics of glyptodonts?
2. Ask your teacher for permission and then e-mail an expert at a local university or at the natural history museum to identify resources.
3. Gather the information from several resources.
4. Take notes using the chart on the back.

More steps are on the back...

© Prufrock Press Inc. • *Independent Study Program*

Resource Card 22b

	Book #1	Book #2	Book #3	Expert Interview
How is the name spelled?	glyptodon	glyptodont	glyptodont	glyptodont
When did the glyptodont live?				
Where did it live?				
How did it protect itself?				

5. Summarize how each of the resources answers your questions.
6. Identify the information that is the same across all of your resources.
   - Fact: Glyptodont is spelled with a *t* at the end of the word.
   - Incorrect information or an opinion: Glyptodon is not spelled with a *t* at the end of the word.
7. Present your information to the class.

© Prufrock Press Inc. • *Independent Study Program*

Resource Card 23

Using a Study Method—Descriptive Study

How do I use the descriptive study method to describe something with numbers and facts?

1. Ask a question that can be answered with numbers or facts about the topic.
2. Decide if you are going to use information that is already known or get new information.
3. You can find old information in various resources, including:
   - books;
   - magazines;
   - newspapers;
   - encyclopedias;
   - films, filmstrips;
   - old documents, records;
   - movies;
   - TV shows;
   - CDs;
   - DVDs; and
   - the Internet.

More steps are on the back...

© Prufrock Press Inc. • *Independent Study Program*

Resource Card 23b

4. You can get new information by doing interviews, surveys, or experiments.
5. Develop a form to collect the data (i.e., numbers, information).
6. If you are collecting new information, you will want to make sure that the information is objective. To make sure it is objective, identify persons who represent the population and identify an observation or data collection method that tries to collect nonbiased information.
7. Gather the information.
8. Identify which information is based on facts and which information is based on opinion.
9. Summarize the notes.
10. Present the information to other people.

Example is on the next Resource Card...

© Prufrock Press Inc. • *Independent Study Program*

Resource Card 24

Using a Study Method—Descriptive Study Example

Example: How do I use the descriptive study method to describe something with numbers and facts?

1. Question: How many students in our school have pets? What kind of pets do they have?
2. Decide on the definition of a *pet*. Identify the kinds of pets that you will include in the survey. Decide if you will include all of the students in the school or just select a sample.
3. Call the Humane Society to see if they have ever conducted a pet survey and ask if they might have suggestions of the types of questions that would be interesting to include. Read about pets to make sure that you have included all of the necessary information.
4. Develop a survey to collect the information.
5. Identify the students in school who will participate in the survey. Ask if they will be willing to participate. Find a time to ask the questions.

More steps are on the back...

© Prufrock Press Inc. • *Independent Study Program*

Appendix D: Resource Cards and Student Booklet Thumbnails

Resource Card 24b

6. Ask each student the questions on the survey.
7. Summarize the information. Identify the number of students who own pets. Identify the different kinds of pets. Identify any differences between boys and girls, between grade levels, and between ages.
8. Share the results with participating classes.

Resource Card 25 — Using a Study Method–Historical Study

How do I use an historical study method to look at the past or history of my topic?

1. Ask a question that can be answered by looking at the past or history of the topic.
2. Look for both primary and secondary sources. In primary sources, the author has directly observed the historical event. In secondary sources, the author reports the observations of others who witnessed the event.
3. You can find information in various resources, including:
   - people who observed the historical event;
   - historians at colleges and universities;
   - historical societies;
   - museums;
   - old documents or records;
   - books;
   - magazines;
   - newspapers;
   - encyclopedias;
   - films or filmstrips;
   - movies;
   - TV shows;
   - CDs;
   - DVDs; and
   - the Internet.

More steps are on the back...

Resource Card 25b

4. Take notes from the resources.
5. Examine the resources and your notes. Make sure that the resources are authentic: would the author have a motive or a bias to exaggerate, distort, or overlook information?
6. Decide which information is based on facts and which information is based on opinion.
7. Summarize the notes.
8. Present the information to other people. Be sure to include the names of all of the resources you used and tell how you decided whether or not they were authentic.

Example is on the next Resource Card...

Resource Card 26 — Using a Study Method–Historical Study Example

Example: How do I use an historical study method to look at the past or history of my topic?

1. Question: How did the different schools in our town get their names?
2. Call the principals of different schools in the area. Identify (living) people, who were either at the school building when it was dedicated, or who know the person or place for which the school was named (primary sources).
3. Go to the library, locate old newspapers, and search on the Internet. Find articles and/or stories about the persons and/or places for which the schools were named (secondary sources).
4. Take notes from the secondary resources. Interview the primary sources.
5. Examine the interviews and your notes. Identify those persons who might tend to exaggerate information or who might be biased in some way.

More steps are on the back...

Resource Card 26b

6. Decide which information is based on facts and which information is based on opinion.
7. Summarize your notes. Identify how school names are often chosen. Identify the number of schools that were named after school leaders, community leaders, historical people, and the like.
8. Present the information to other people. Be sure to include the names of all of the resources you used and tell how you decided whether or not they were authentic.

Resource Card 27 — Using a Study Method–Developmental Study

How do I use a developmental study method to look at the changes or development of my topic?

1. Ask about a change or the development of a topic over time.
2. Examine how other people have looked at a change or the development of the topic in the past.
3. You can find how others have looked at change by:
   - interviewing experts;
   - writing letters or e-mails to people who are interested in the topic; and
   - reading books, magazines, journals, newspapers, Web sites, and encyclopedias.
4. Design a way for you to look at a change or the development of the topic.
5. There are various ways to study change. You can give a test or questionnaire at the beginning and end of an activity and look at the differences, or you can observe something every day and graph or chart the information.

More steps are on the back...

Resource Card 27b

6. Collect the data.
7. Summarize the data.
8. Present the information to other people. Be sure to include how others have observed changes in the topic, how you decided to observe changes, and the results of what you observed.

Example is on the next Resource Card...

Resource Card 28 — Using a Study Method–Developmental Study Example

Example: How do I use a developmental study method to look at the changes or development of my topic?

1. Question: What are my classmates' attitudes toward school throughout the year? Do they change? Do they remain the same?
2. Ask your teacher how other people have looked at attitudes.
3. Interview, e-mail, or write letters to educators at colleges and universities. Look in magazines, journals, and the Internet to see how others have looked at attitudes.
4. Define *attitude*. Identify the opinions you will want to collect. Design a form to measure these attitudes.
5. With your teacher, decide on the same time each day that you will collect the data. Explain the form to your classmates.

More steps are on the back...

Resource Card 28b

6. Collect the data.
7. Summarize the data.
   - Did the attitudes change from the beginning of the year to the end of the year?
   - Did the attitudes change according to the day?
   - Did the attitudes change depending upon what was being studied?
   - Were there differences between boys and girls?
8. Present the results to the class. Be sure to include how others have observed attitudes and how you decided to observe attitudes.

© Prufrock Press Inc. • *Independent Study Program*

Resource Card 29 — Using a Study Method–Case Study

How do I use a case study method to closely observe a person, group, or something?

1. Ask a question that requires you to closely observe a person, group, place, or thing.
2. Examine how other people have looked at the person, group, place, or thing.
3. You can find how others have looked at the person, group, or thing by:
   - interviewing experts;
   - writing letters or e-mails to people who are interested in the topic; and
   - reading books, magazines, journals, newspapers, and Internet sites.
4. If you are going to observe a person or group, find a person who is willing to let you observe him or her. If you are going to observe a place or thing, locate it and get permission to observe it.
5. Design a way to observe the person, group, or thing. Decide how long you will observe, how you will take notes (e.g., in a journal, an interview, on cards, on tape).

More steps are on the back…

© Prufrock Press Inc. • *Independent Study Program*

Resource Card 29b

6. Collect the data by observing the person, group, or thing.
7. Summarize the data.
8. Present the information to other people. Tell them why you decided to observe this person, group, or thing; how you conducted your observation; and what you learned.

Example is on the next Resource Card…

© Prufrock Press Inc. • *Independent Study Program*

Resource Card 30 — Using a Study Method–Case Study Example

Example: How do I use a case study method to closely observe a person, group, or something?

1. Question: How does a principal spend his or her time during the school day?
2. Identify when you will observe and how you will collect information. You will probably want to use notes, as well as a tape or video recorder.
3. Find a principal who is willing to let you observe him or her. Ask the principal what he or she does during a typical school day.
4. Design a form that you will use in taking notes. You will want to have a way of recording the time and place of the principal's activity.
5. Observe the principal during a week's period of time. His or her activity will probably change from day to day and from week to week.

More steps are on the back…

© Prufrock Press Inc. • *Independent Study Program*

Resource Card 30b

6. Look at notes and summarize the data. Name the different types of activities in which the principal participated, and find the average amount of time that he or she spent on various activities.
7. Present the information to your principal, teacher, and classmates. Tell them how you collected the information.

© Prufrock Press Inc. • *Independent Study Program*

Resource Card 31 — Using a Study Method–Correlation Study

How do I use the correlation study method to relate one thing with another thing using numbers?

1. Ask a question that requires you to compare one thing with another thing using numbers.
2. Describe each thing that you are going to compare. Look at how others have described these things and how they have measured or studied them.
3. Decide what or who will be in the study. Remember to select a sample that represents the general population and is not biased.
4. Decide how you will measure each thing that you are going to compare:
   - Will you look at tests?
   - Will you observe how they grow?
   - Will you get information from newspapers or the Internet?
5. Collect the data.

More steps are on the back…

© Prufrock Press Inc. • *Independent Study Program*

Resource Card 31b

6. Put the data about one item on a line graph. Put the data about the other item on a separate line graph or a separate line on the same graph. Compare the two items.
7. Analyze the data on the graph.
   - If the two lines go up or down in the same way (i.e., are parallel), the items are related. When one item occurs, the other will probably happen.
   - If one line goes down and one line goes up, the items are inversely related. When one item occurs, the other will probably not happen.
   - If the lines don't look like the described situations, the items probably are not related.
8. Share the information with other people.

Example is on the next Resource Card…

© Prufrock Press Inc. • *Independent Study Program*

Resource Card 32 — Using a Study Method–Correlation Study Example

Example: How do I use the correlation study method to relate one thing with another thing using numbers?

1. Question: Is there a relationship between the number of study hours at home and grades?
2. Look at how others have studied this relationship. Ask students and teachers in your school. Ask or e-mail experts at local colleges and universities.
3. Define what you mean by *study hours* and *grades*.
4. Decide what subject area you will study and who will be in your study.
5. Decide how you will measure study hours and grades. Develop a form that the participants can use at home and find a satisfactory way to collect test grades.
6. Find the students who are willing to participate in your study. Have them collect the data for one semester.

More steps are on the back…

© Prufrock Press Inc. • *Independent Study Program*

Appendix D: Resource Cards and Student Booklet Thumbnails

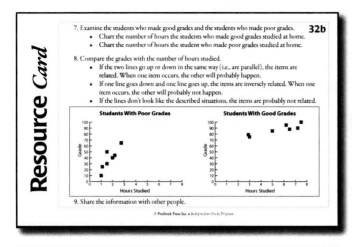

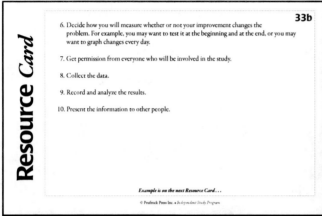

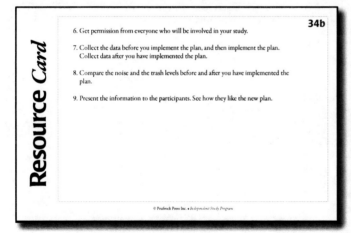

Resource Card 36b

5. Decide how you will measure "similar words in spelling lists and in writing sentences" and "spelling lists." You might decide to use the spelling lists and sentences from the spelling book with one group having access to the book and the other group not having access to the book.
6. Identify how you are going to collect the data.
7. Conduct the experiment for at least 3 weeks.
8. Summarize the data. Show the number of words spelled correctly by each group on a graph and/or on a chart.
9. Present the information to the class.

Resource Card 37 — Using a Study Method–Research Designs

What are some different research designs?

1. One design involves both experimental group(s) and control group(s).
   - In this design, select two groups.
   - Give both groups a pretest and both groups a posttest.
   - Give only one group the treatment (i.e., the experimental group).
   - Compare the differences between groups on the posttest to see if the treatment made a change in the experimental group.

This design can be varied by adding more experimental groups or more control groups. In this way, more treatments or more control variables can be tested.

More steps are on the back...

Resource Card 37b

2. Another research design is the time-series design, used with one or more groups.
   - In this design, select one or more groups.
   - Give the group(s) several tests over a period of time to eliminate the possibility that the change was influenced one time only.
   - Administer a treatment.
   - After the treatment, give several posttests over a period of time. Again, you can see the effect of time on the treatment.

There are many more research designs. Ask your teacher, talk to researchers, or look in different resources for more ideas.

Resource Card 38 — Using a Study Method–Nonbiased Samples

How do I get a nonbiased sample?

1. Decide what population is needed for the study.
2. There are several ways to select a sample:
   - Draw names from a hat.
   - Take every third (or some other number) name from an alphabetical list.
   - Use a table of random numbers.
3. Try to avoid volunteers who may bias the sample. For example, you may be wondering what TV shows fifth-grade students in your school like. You know that there are an equal number of boys and girls in the five fifth-grade classes, so you want to ask an equal number of boys and girls from all of the classes to complete the survey. If you get responses from students in your class who volunteer to answer the questions, you will only know what they think—not what students from different classes might think. If you ask for volunteers, you might not get an equal of number of boys and girls to respond to your survey. If the percentage of boys and girls who answer your survey about their favorite TV show is not similar to the percentage of boys and girls in the entire fifth grade, then there will be bias in your survey results.

Example is on the back...

Resource Card 38b

Examples

1. Call every 10th name in the school phone book and ask opinions.
2. Put all of the eighth-grade students' names in a hat and select 50 for the study.
3. Get an alphabetical list of the students in the school. Use a set of random numbers to select 100 of the students. (Random number lists can be found in statistics books.)

Resource Card 39 — Collecting Information–Overview

Resources for Information
- Internet
- electronic sources
- objects for experiments
- people
- places
- print/text

How to Organize Information
- classifying
- outlining
- summarizing
- taking notes
- using index cards
- webbing

Ways to Collect Information
- conducting an experiment
- corresponding by letter or e-mail
- interviewing
- observing
- reading
- searching the Internet
- conducting a survey

Resource Card 40 — Collecting Information–Resources

Although there are endless places to collect information, these fall into a few basic categories:

- *Internet:* Web pages that contain relevant information
- *Electronic sources:* CDs, DVDs, e-mail, electronic encyclopedias, videos, and TV programs
- *Objects for experiments:* items that will be observed or manipulated when testing different hypotheses
- *People:* experts who can be interviewed in person, by phone, or e-mail or letter
- *Places:* specific locations, such as museums, cemeteries, buildings, and historical sites
- *Print/Texts:* books, magazines, newspapers, journals, newsletters, and documents

Resource Card 41 — Collecting Information–Index

There are many different ways to collect information.

	Card Numbers
Conducting an Experiment (see Resource Cards 35–36)	
Corresponding by Letter or E-mail	42–46
Interviewing	47–49
Reading	50
Observing	51–52
Searching the Internet	53
Conducting a Survey	54–60

Appendix D: Resource Cards and Student Booklet Thumbnails

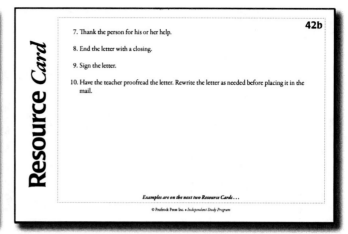
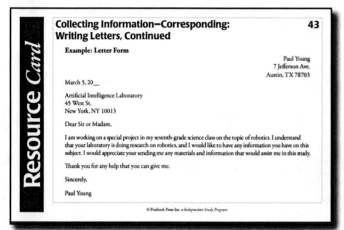
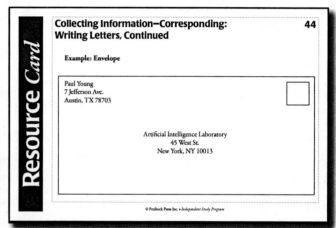
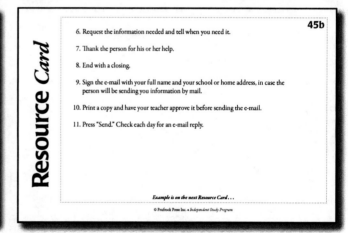
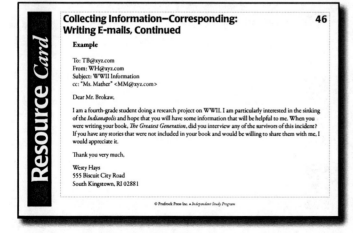
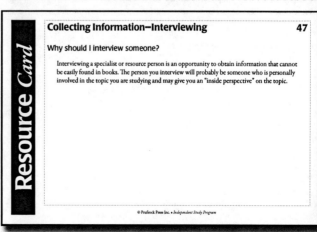

Resource Card 48: Collecting Information–Interviewing, Continued

How do I interview?

1. Before the interview:
   - Select a person who knows about the subject you are studying.
   - Call or write the person to set up an interview. Be persistent; you may have to talk with several people before you reach the person you want to interview. Always give your name, who you are (a student and give your school name), what you are studying, and why you want to interview the person.
   - Make an appointment. Give the person an estimate of the amount of time that you will need for the interview (try not to take more than 30 minutes). Be flexible and work around the person's schedule as much as possible. Write down the date, place, and time you will meet, and repeat this information back to the person before completing the conversation.
   - Do your homework. It is important to know who the person is, why he or she might be helpful to you, and learn something about the interviewee before the interview.
   - Make some notes to take into the interview. These should include the name of the person being interviewed, date and time of the interview, position or occupation of the person, why this person was selected, the topic that will be discussed, and background information on the person.
   - Write a list of questions you would like to ask the person.

   More steps are on the back...

Resource Card 48b

2. During the interview:
   - When you meet the person, introduce yourself, shake hands, and thank him or her for giving you the interview.
   - If you wish to tape record the interview, ask the person for permission.
   - Ask the questions from the list, but don't limit yourself to the list. If the person is talking about something of interest, ask follow-up questions. Much of our most interesting information comes from spontaneous communication.
   - Be a good listener; look directly at the person.
   - Listen for clue words and phrases that tell you something important is coming.
   - Take a few notes about important information.
   - Allow a few seconds of silent time after the person stops talking. Allow time for the person to think through responses and perhaps add more information.
   - Try to visualize or see pictures in your mind.
   - Keep to the time limit. If you told the person that the interview would be no more than 30 minutes, be sure to stop right before the time limit to wrap up the interview. If the person wants and is able to spend more time with you, he or she will let you know.
   - When the interview is finished, thank the person again and express that he or she has been very helpful to you in your study.

   More steps are on the next Resource Card...

Resource Card 49: Collecting Information–Interviewing, Continued

3. After the interview:
   - Review the notes and tape recording (if applicable) as soon as possible while the information is fresh on your mind.
   - Write the interview in paragraph form to include in the report.
   - Write the interviewed person a thank-you note, telling how much you appreciate the time that was spent helping you with your research project.
   - If possible, send the person a copy of the report you write or invite him or her to view the product when you present it to class.

Resource Card 50: Collecting Information–Reading

How do I collect information from print materials?

1. Look up information by examining the table of contents and the index in the book. If the resource is an encyclopedia or other type of reference material, look at the guide letters on the outside of the book or at the top of the pages.

2. Examine many resources and select the ones that best relate to your questions.

3. Keep the study questions in mind and focus on the readings that help answer the question. Avoid getting sidetracked by interesting but unrelated information.

4. Mark important information with sticky notes or tabs that are color-coded to match your questions.

5. Write down key words or the main ideas on the sticky notes to help you remember what is important in the paragraph.

More steps are on the back...

Resource Card 50b

6. Take notes of important information using your computer, cards, or paper (see Taking Notes, Resource Card 68).

7. Whenever you write a note, remember to note the source (e.g., where you find the information—the author(s), the name of the book, the page numbers, the publisher, and the city where it was published).

Resource Card 51: Collecting Information–Observing

How do I observe a person, place, or thing?

1. Identify the important characteristics of what you want to observe. Do you want to observe its physical features (size, shape, color, texture, weight), how it sounds, feels, changes, and grows, or something else?

2. Identify how long you are going to observe. Are you going to observe the person, place, or object for 30 minutes? An hour? Every day? Once a week? At what time? In the morning? In the evening? It's important for scientists to make their observations consistent—same length of time, same time of day, and same day.

3. Identify if you are going to make any changes to the person, place, or object. For example, you might want to add flowers to your backyard and see if it attracts different types of birds. If you do, then you will want to observe before you make the change, during the change, and after the change.

More steps are on the back...

Resource Card 51b

4. Identify how you will collect notes. Will you write in a journal? Will you talk into a tape recorder? Will you use a computer?

5. Once these decisions are made, you are ready to begin your observations.

6. Collect the data as you observe the person, place, or thing.

7. Summarize the data.

Example is on the next Resource Card...

Resource Card 52: Collecting Information–Observing, Continued

Example: How do I observe a person, place, or thing?

1. Question: What are the feeding habits of hummingbirds?

2. I want to observe how many times and how long these birds stay at the hummingbird feeder in my backyard.

3. I'm going to observe the hummingbird feeder between 6:30–7:30 a.m. and 5–6 p.m. each day for 3 days for one week.

4. I'm going to add some flowers that hummingbirds like during the second week and observe them again at the same times for 3 days.

5. I'm going to take the flowers away during the third week and observe them again at the same times for 3 days.

More steps are on the back...

Appendix D: Resource Cards and Student Booklet Thumbnails

Resource Card 52b

6. I will collect notes in a journal. I will make notes of the types of hummingbirds, how frequently they visit the feeder, and how long they stay (using a stopwatch).

7. I observed using this form:

Date and Time	Type	Frequency of Visit	Length of Visit
5/16 (6:30–7:30 a.m.)	Ruby Throat	✓	10 seconds
		✓	8 seconds

8. I summarized my data using a graph (see Resource Cards 86–91).

Resource Card 53 — Collecting Information—Searching the Internet

How do I collect information using the Internet?

1. Decide on some key words and phrases from your topic that you can search.

2. Select a search engine. When the "Search" box appears, type in one of your key words or phrases. Hit "Enter."

3. You will see a listing of the results of your search. These may be arranged in different orders, depending on the search engine you use. Typically they are listed in terms of relevancy, with the most relevant item appearing first. Read over the descriptions of the sites and click on one that sounds helpful.

4. Review the Web page. If it is helpful, take notes or print it. If you need to research other sites, return to the listing and click on another choice.

5. You may choose to search for another key word or phrase to gather even more information. Follow the same process.

6. To cite the reference, write down the Web address and the title and author if there is one.

Resource Card 54 — Collecting Information—Conducting a Survey

What is a survey?

A survey is a way of examining what a group of people thinks about something. The surveyor must find an appropriate group and develop questions that will allow the people surveyed to give facts or express opinions.

How do I survey a group of people?

1. Develop questions that allow the people to give facts or express their opinions (see Resource Card 55).
2. Decide how to collect the information (see Resource Card 56).
3. Select an nonbiased sample (see Resource Card 38).
4. Conduct the survey (see Resource Card 57).
5. Analyze the results of the study (see Resource Card 58).
6. Report the results (see Resource Card 60).

Resource Card 55 — Collecting Information—Conducting a Survey, Continued

How do I develop questions that give facts or allow people to express opinions?

1. Gather background information. Background information tells you about the people who are completing the survey. This information on a person can be as important to your survey as the person's opinions.

Possible Background Information

Name_____ Age_____ Sex_____
Occupation_____ Ethnicity_____
School_____ Grade_____
City_____ State_____

Note: Decide which information is important to your survey. You may not need to use all of the items found on the Background Information sheet above.

More steps are on the back . . .

Resource Card 55b

2. Formulate your questions in one of the following ways.

- *Open-ended format*
  How do you feel about the food in the school cafeteria?

- *Choice format*
  Do you like the food in the school cafeteria?
  Yes ❑   No ❑

- *Rating scale*
  How do you rate the food in the school cafeteria?
  Extremely Delicious ❑   Somewhat Delicious ❑   Not Delicious ❑

  How often do you purchase the food in the school cafeteria?
  Always ❑   Frequently ❑   Sometimes ❑   Never ❑

Resource Card 56 — Collecting Information—Conducting a Survey

How do I decide how to collect the information?

The answers to the survey questions may be obtained in several ways:
- in person,
- by telephone, and
- through written format such as by mail or a handout.

Resource Card 57 — Collecting Information—Conducting a Survey, Continued

How do I conduct a survey?

1. Make copies of the questionnaire for each person who will be surveyed (use one questionnaire per person).

2. Ensure that each person receives his or her questionnaire. If you distribute or mail the questionnaire, include written directions informing people what to do and how to return the information to you.

3. It is practically impossible to have all of your questionnaires returned. However, the more that are returned, the better the survey results will be.

4. When the questionnaires are returned, you may begin to analyze the results (see next Resource Card).

Resource Card 58 — Collecting Information—Conducting a Survey, Continued

How do I analyze the results of the study?

1. Look back at the questions asked on the survey and write these on paper.

2. Tally the information from the questionnaire in several ways in order to answer all of the questions.

3. Write an answer for each of the questions.

4. Think about other questions that may have come to mind that you wonder about and might like to answer at another time.

Example is on the next Resource Card . . .

Resource Card 59: Collecting Information—Conducting a Survey, Continued

Example

1. Isabel wanted to do a survey in her school about pets and wanted to find answers to the following questions:
   - How many students in my school own pets?
   - What kinds of pets do they have?
   - How many pets do they have?
   - Which grade has more pets?
   - Do more boys or girls own pets?

2. Because it would be too difficult and too costly to survey all of the students in the school, Isabel selected two grade levels as the sample.

3. Isabel decided to distribute the questionnaire to all fifth- and seventh-grade teachers and ask them to have their classes complete the survey within the next week.

More steps are on the back...

Resource Card 59b

4. Isabel picked up the completed questionnaires from the teachers after one week. She knew that it would be impossible to have all of the questionnaires returned, and she was excited to have approximately 70% of them returned.

5. Isabel looked back at the questions she had asked at the beginning of the survey.

6. Isabel tallied the information from the questionnaire in several ways:
   - number and kind of pets fifth graders reported,
   - number and kind of pets seventh graders reported,
   - number and kind of pets reported in all,
   - number and kind of pets males reported, and
   - number and kind of pets females reported.

7. Isabel wrote an answer to each of the five questions asked and decided that the best way to show the results was by using a graph.

8. Isabel then thought about other questions and wondered if the results would have been different in a school from a different part of the country. She wondered if her friend from another state would like to do the same survey and compare results.

Example is on the next Resource Card...

Resource Card 60: Collecting Information—Conducting a Survey, Continued

Example

Pet Survey

Grade Level _____   Sex: ☐ Male ☐ Female

How many pets do you have? Write the number on the line.
_____ dogs
_____ cats
_____ turtles
_____ fish
_____ horses
_____ birds
_____ other (be specific) _____

Graph of results is on the back...

Resource Card 60b

Graph of Survey Results

[Bar graph showing Pets Owned by Fifth Graders and Pets Owned by Seventh Graders, with Number of Pets on y-axis (0–60) and Kind of Pets on x-axis: Dogs, Cats, Turtles, Fish, Horses, Birds, Other]

Resource Card 61: Collecting Information—Organizing Information: Index

Once you have found information in various resources, you will need to organize it. There are several ways to organize information:

Card Numbers

- *Classifying*—organizing items into groups that are alike in some way. 62
- *Outlining*—taking notes using a structured system of listing main ideas and supporting details. 63
- *Summarizing*—sorting through a large amount of information and putting the main ideas into a shortened form that is easy to understand. 64–67
- *Taking notes*—recording important information gathered from your readings. . 68–70
- *Using index cards*—taking notes by using a system of note cards or index cards. Each card has notes about one resource with citations and brief ideas. 71
- *Webbing*—organizing ideas by topics and subtopics or by concepts, generalizations, principles, and theories by connecting related ideas with lines. It looks like a spider web. 72

Resource Card 62: Collecting Information—Organizing Information: Classifying

How do I classify?

Classify means to organize items into groups. Each group is alike in some way.

1. Think of all of the ways the set of items are alike (e.g., color, size, use, type).
2. Decide on a few headings that describe the characteristics.
3. Make a chart with each heading across the top.
4. List the items under the headings where they best fit.

Example is on the back...

Resource Card 62b

Example

Items: drums, violin, guitar, flute, trumpet, piano, bongo, cymbal, clarinet, tambourine, banjo, trombone, harp

Classify the set of examples above.

1. Think of ways the above items are alike: musical instruments, percussion, stringed, wind.
2. Decide on appropriate headings: percussion, stringed, wind instruments.
3. Make a chart to show the categories.
4. List each item under the appropriate heading.

Musical Instruments		
Percussion	Stringed	Wind
drums	violin	flute
bongo	guitar	trumpet
cymbal	banjo	clarinet
piano	harp	trombone
tambourine		

Resource Card 63: Collecting Information—Organizing Information: Outlining

How do I outline?

1. Select a book, chapter, film, or your notes to outline.
2. Determine the main ideas. They will be written beside the Roman numerals.
3. List the first main idea beside I.
4. List supporting ideas under I beside A., B., C., and so on. Always indent the letters.
5. Continue this procedure for II. with the second main idea.
6. Use words and phrases, not sentences.
7. If you will be researching other sources, you may leave space to fill in later.

Example is on the back...

Appendix D: Resource Cards and Student Booklet Thumbnails

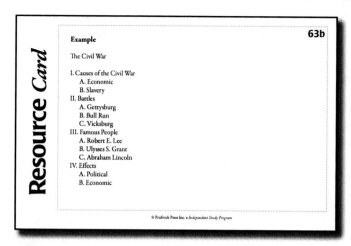

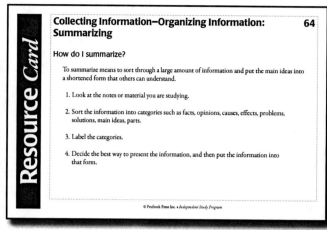

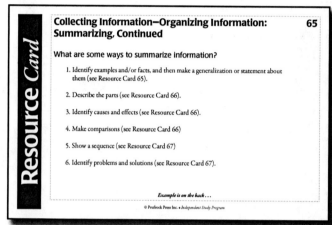

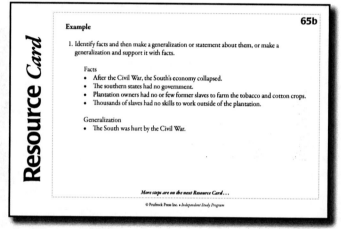

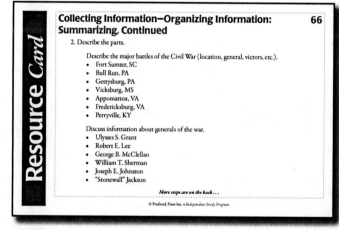

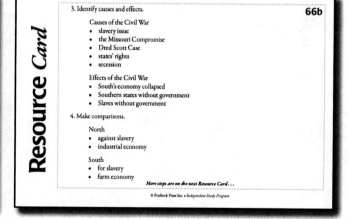

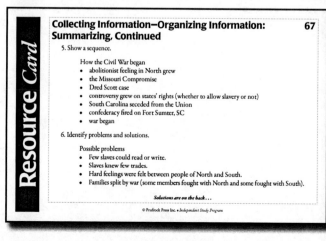

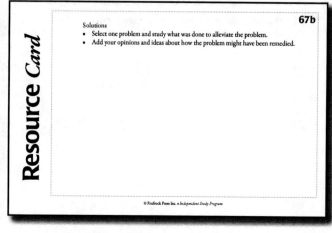

Collecting Information—Organizing Information: Taking Notes — 68

What is note taking?

Note taking is a way of recording important information you gather from books, magazines, films, and interviews. There are several ways to take notes, including outlining and using note cards.

Note-Taking Tips:
1. Use your own words as much as possible. Avoid copying directly from the source.
2. If you do copy directly from the source, use quotation marks so that you know it is a quote. You will either reword the ideas when you write the report or use the information as a direct quote. Remember to also record where you found the quote so you don't forget. If it was found in a book, write down the exact page number(s) on which the quote appeared.
3. Spend most of your time reading and only a small amount of time writing.
4. Reread your notes as soon as possible in order to fill in any gaps.

Collecting Information—Organizing Information: Taking Notes, Continued — 69

How do I take notes?

1. Before note taking:
    - Have materials ready—paper or note cards and a pencil or pen.
    - Look over the material you will be studying and decide how you want to take notes—outlining, note cards, or your own method.
    - Always list the source on your paper or note card—title of source, author, publisher, city of publication, and date.

2. During note taking:
    - Use headings or main topics.
    - Use abbreviations.
    - Write a question mark (?) when you don't understand something or need information.
    - Use symbols to emphasize important information, such as underlining, circling, or making check marks.
    - This is a rough draft, so don't waste time erasing. Cross out instead.
    - Look for signal words for clues about important information (see back of this card).

Example is on the back...

Example: Signal Words — 69b

Support Signals	Conclusion Signals
for example	therefore
for instance	finally
first, second, third	in conclusion
similarly	as a result
most important	in summary
a major development	from this we see
again, next, then	hence
consequently	thus
another	
also	
furthermore	
likewise	
in addition	
equally important	
whereas	

Collecting Information—Organizing Information: Taking Notes, Continued — 70

How do I take notes?

3. After note taking:
    - Reread notes as soon as possible while the information is still fresh in your mind.
    - Try to fill in any question marks (?) you have by asking questions or finding another source.
    - Rewrite any parts that don't make sense.

Collecting Information—Organizing Information: Using Index Cards — 71

How do I use an index card?

1. Write the study question at the top of each index card.
2. Select a book, chapter, or film from which to take notes.
3. List the following information on the index card:
    - title of book, chapter, or film (or other source);
    - author(s);
    - publisher and city and state where it was published;
    - copyright date; and
    - page numbers where information was found.
4. Write any information on the card that pertains to the study question or note a particular aspect of the book. You may find many pieces of interesting information, but list only the information that helps to answer the study question.

Example is on the back...

Example — 71b

Jeffrey, G., & Ganeri, A. (2005). *Cleopatra: The life of an Egyptian queen.* New York: Rosen Publishing.

Good resource for the important events in Cleopatra's life.

Collecting Information—Organizing Information: Webbing — 72

How do I web?

1. Write the main topic in the middle of your paper and draw a circle around it.
2. Write subtopics from each of your questions in circles around the main topic.
3. Draw lines from the main topic to the subtopics.
4. Add lines from each of the subtopic circles that might describe parts, stages, habits, or any of the descriptions that are mentioned on Resource Card 11 or in your resources.
5. Continue in this way until all of the information that you have gathered or organized appears in your web.

Example is on the back...

Example — 72b

Below is a web of a character analysis of Sal from *Walk Two Moons* by Sharon Creech

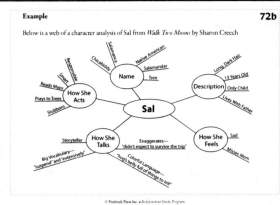

Appendix D: Resource Cards and Student Booklet Thumbnails

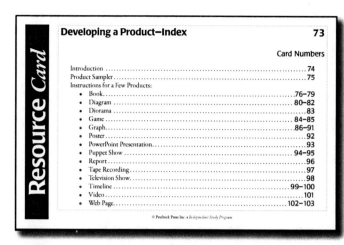

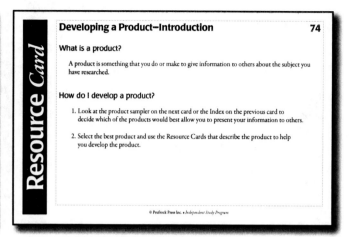

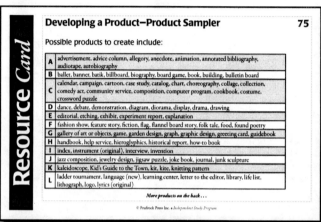

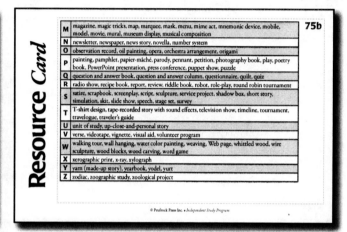

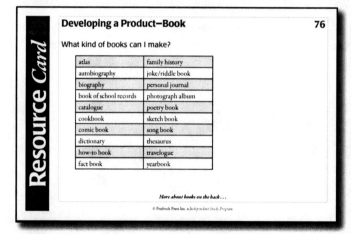

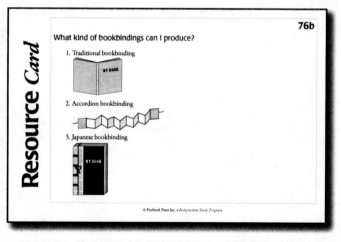

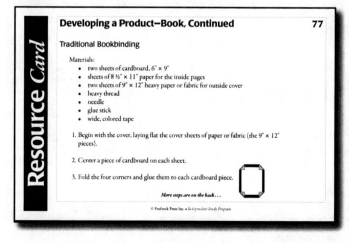

Resource Card 78: Developing a Product—Book, Continued

Accordion Binding

Materials:
- two 5 ½"-square pieces of cardboard
- two 7"-square pieces of heavy paper or fabric
- one strip of 5" × 30" paper
- glue stick

1. Center each piece of cardboard on the heavy paper or fabric. (Follow the illustrated example on Resource Card 77.)
2. Fold the four corners of the paper or fabric and glue them to each cardboard piece (see Resource Card 77, step 3 for a diagram).
3. Fold the edges and glue them to each cardboard piece (see Resource Card 77, step 4 for a diagram).

More steps are on the back...

Resource Card 78b

4. Fold the strip of 5" × 30" paper back and forth every 5 inches. It should look like an accordion.
5. Glue one end of the folded strip of paper to the inside of the front cover. Glue the other end of the paper to the inside of the back cover.
6. The book is ready to fill with drawings, writings, pictures, and anything else you can imagine.

Resource Card 79: Developing a Product—Book

Japanese Bookbinding

Materials:
- two 5 ½" × 1 ½" pieces of cardboard
- two 7" × 8" pieces of colored paper for outside cover
- sheets of 5 ½" × 8" pieces of paper for inside pages
- hole punch
- glue stick
- 40" piece of yarn
- embroidery needle

1. Lay the 7" × 8" pieces of heavy paper or fabric flat on the table. If your paper or fabric has a design on it, be sure to put that face down. (Follow the illustrated example on Resource Card 77 to complete the next three steps.)
2. Center the pieces of cardboard on each sheet of heavy paper or fabric.
3. Fold the four corners of the paper or fabric and glue them to each cardboard piece.
4. Fold the edges and glue them to each cardboard piece.

More steps are on the back...

Resource Card 79b

5. Measure and mark four even dots down the middle of the covered cardboard.
6. Punch holes at each dot.
7. Put the top and bottom covered cardboard pieces on the left side of the stack of paper for the inside of the book.
8. Mark the paper where the holes in the cover are and punch holes in the paper.
9. Thread yard into the embroidery needle and sew according to the directions below. Tie a bow on the front.

Directions for Binding:
1. Down at B (keep several inches out in order to tie a bow at the end), and then go around the side and back down at B.
2. Up at A, go around the side and up again at A.
3. Around the top and up again at A.
4. Down at B.
5. Up again at C, go around the side and up again at C.
6. Down at D, go around the side and down again at D.
7. Go around the bottom and down again at D.
8. Up at C. Tied in a bow.

Resource Card 80: Developing a Product—Diagram

What is a diagram?

A diagram is a graphic design or drawing that helps explain:
- the parts of an object, or
- the steps or stages of something.

How do I make a diagram?

1. Decide what size the design should be.
   - Should it be large enough to present in a class presentation?
   - Should it fill a page in a written report?
   - Should it be small enough to insert in the text of a written report?
2. Make a rough sketch of the diagram on a scratch piece of paper.
   - If drawing is difficult for you, trace the picture from a book.
   - If the drawing in the book is too small, use an opaque projector to enlarge it. Ask a teacher for assistance.

More steps are on the back...

Resource Card 80b

3. When you are satisfied with the sketch, draw it again on poster board or good paper.
4. Use a ruler and pencil to make lines to the parts of the figure you will explain.
5. Print the words in pencil next to the line.
6. When the diagram is complete, use pens, crayons, or felt markers to color it and make it attractive.

Note: If you are not an artist, you may want to find a diagram on the Internet. For example, go to a search engine such as Google, and enter "flower diagram." A variety of diagrams will appear that you might be able to use in your presentation. You can also ask your teacher what computer software might be used for drawing diagrams such as Inspiration™ or SmartDraw™.

Resource Card 81: Developing a Product—Diagram, Continued

Example

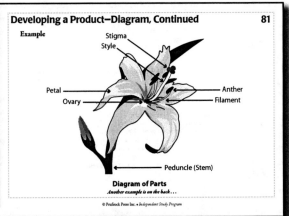

Diagram of Parts

Another example is on the back...

Resource Card 81b

Example

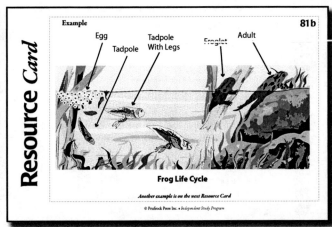

Frog Life Cycle

Another example is on the next Resource Card

Appendix D: Resource Cards and Student Booklet Thumbnails

Developing a Product—Diagram, Continued 82

Example

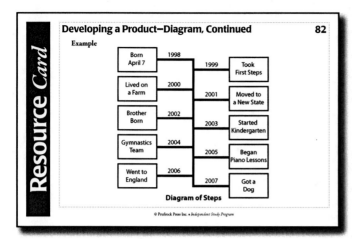

Diagram of Steps

Developing a Product—Diorama 83

What is a diorama?

A diorama is a box that contains objects of models that depict a scene.

How do I make a diorama?

Materials:
- cardboard box
- paper
- paints, crayons, or felt markers
- various objects or models

Steps are on the back...

83b

1. Plan how the diorama will look.
   - How large is the box? Measure the inside of the box.
   - Review your question. Identify what people, places, and/or objects will need to be included to answer your question. For example, if your question asks about the habitat of the dinosaur, you will want to consider the vegetation, the presence of other animals, and the climate and topography of the earth during that time period. Given the size of the box, how large should all of these items be?
   - What background scene do you want? On scratch paper, make a rough sketch of the background scene to fit inside of the box.
   - What objects of models will best depict the scene? Collect or color these.

2. Create the diorama.
   - Cut paper the same size as the inside of the box.
   - Draw the background scene from the rough sketch; color or paint it.
   - When it is dry, glue or tape the scene to the inside of the box.
   - Arrange the objects or models in the box.

3. Explain what the diorama depicts.
   - Write a description of the scene to tell others about it.
   - Label the objects or parts, if necessary.

Developing a Product—Game 84

How do I make a board game?

Materials:
- poster board
- pencils and markers
- glue
- box
- buttons, paper clips, colored circles
- various colors of construction paper
- dice (optional)
- 3" × 5" index cards
- scissors

1. Plan and design the board game.
   - Think of as many questions as possible about the topic you have studied (at least 30, and the more the better).
   - Make a rough sketch of how you want the board to look (see examples).
   - Make a set of rules for the game, but be sure to keep them simple.

More steps are on the back...

84b

2. Construct the game.
   - Copy the questions on the index cards. Write a question and answer on one side of the card.
   - Make a few risk cards that give directions such as: "Move ahead 3 spaces"; "Lose a turn"; "Take 2 turns"; "Go back to start"; and "Exchange places with someone."
   - Either draw squares or circles on the poster board for the spaces for the markers to move, or cut out squares or circles from construction paper and glue them to the board.
   - Decorate the board with pictures or designs to make it appealing.
   - Collect markers for the players to use, or make them out of colored paper.
   - Write the rules neatly on construction paper and glue them to the back of the game. Consider a variation of some of these rules:
     - The object of the game is to get to the finish before anyone else.
     - Place all players' markers at the start position.
     - Roll a die to see who goes first and continue in a clockwise rotation.
     - Each player rolls the dice and moves the number of spaces indicated. Draw a card and try to answer the question. If correct, move ahead one space. If incorrect, move back a space.
     - If you land on a space with someone else's maker, that person must go back to start.
     - Keep all markers, question cards, and dice in the box.

More steps are on the next Resource Card...

Developing a Product—Game, Continued 85

3. Evaluate the game.
   - When the board game is completed, play it with someone to see if it works. Ask the other player to help you improve it.
   - It is important to consider the following questions: Do you have enough questions? Were the questions too easy or too difficult? Did the game last too long or not long enough? Was it enjoyable?
   - Make the necessary corrections.
   - Explain the game to the class and invite everyone to play.

Example is on the back...

85b

Examples

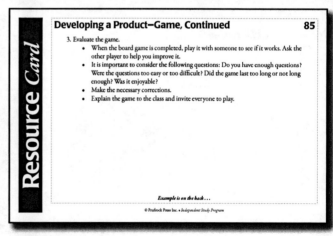

Developing a Product—Graph 86

What is a graph?

A graph is a diagram that shows the relationship between sets of numbers and some other factor. It shows comparisons clearly with a small amount of data.

There are four kinds of graphs discussed in the Resource Cards:
- line graph,
- bar graph,
- pictograph, and
- pie graph.

Developing a Product—Graph, Continued — 87

How do I make a line graph?

Materials:
- two sets of numbers
- graph paper
- ruler
- pencil

1. Plan the information that will go on the graph.
   - Look at the numbers you collected in the study.
   - Decide which information will be placed on the horizontal line and which information will go on the vertical line. (Note: In most studies the time data—days, months, and years—go on the horizontal line.)
   - Decide how many squares on the graph paper will be used for the horizontal and vertical lines of the graph. Try to balance the graph so that the horizontal and vertical lines are approximately the same length.

More steps are on the back...

87b

2. Draw the line on the graph.
   - On graph paper, draw the horizontal and vertical lines, long enough to accommodate the information you are showing.
   - Plot the points on the graph where the horizontal and vertical lines cross (not in the spaces on the graph paper) by penciling a small dot for each piece of information.
   - When all points are plotted, draw a line to connect all of the points.
   - It is possible for the line graph to have more than one line on the same graph. A second set of data can be plotted on the graph for comparison (see example).
   - Label all parts of the graph—title of the graph, vertical axis, horizontal axis, and the line(s) drawn.

Example is on the next Resource Card...

Developing a Product—Graph, Continued — 88

Line Graph Example

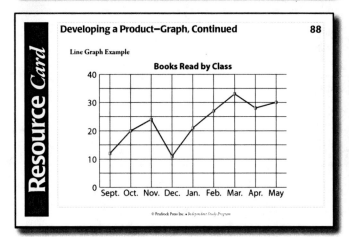

Developing a Product—Graph, Continued — 89

How do I make a bar graph?

Materials:
- two sets of numbers
- graph paper
- ruler
- pencil or colored pencils

1. Follow the steps presented on the Line Graph Resource Card. Instead of placing dots for the data and drawing lines, place a mark and color in the columns or "bars."

2. Bars can be drawn vertically or horizontally.

Example is on the back...

89b

Bar Graph Example

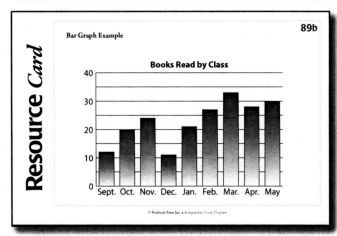

Developing a Product—Graph, Continued — 90

How do I make a pictograph?

Materials:
- two sets of numbers
- ruler
- paper
- pencil

1. Plan the graph.
   - Pictographs are similar to line and bar graphs. However, pictures instead of lines and bars are used to impart information.
   - Choose the pictures you will use to represent the data. Usually pictures are used that reflect the kind of information you are representing. For example, if the graph is about money, a dollar sign ($) or pictures of coins might be used.
   - Decide what each symbol will represent. For example, one coin might represent $100. If you want to show $300 on the graph, three coins would be used. If you wanted to show only $50, then a picture of a half coin would be used.

More steps are on the back...

90b

2. Draw the pictograph.
   - Because each symbol must be the same size, make one symbol and copy or trace it for all of the other symbols. You may either cut them out and paste them on the graph, or you may draw them directly on the graph.
   - As you draw or paste on the symbols, keep them in a straight line or column.
   - Label the graph, including a key that tells what the symbols represent.

Pictograph Example

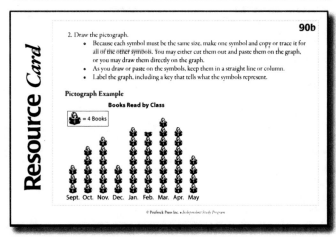

Developing a Product—Graph — 91

How do I make a pie graph?

Materials:
- several sets of numbers and data
- protractor
- compass or round object
- ruler
- unlined paper
- pencil

1. Plan the pie graph.
   - Take each part and convert it into a percentage (i.e., divide one part by the total number of parts). For example, divide the number of books read in one month by the total number of books read in one year to get the percentage read for that month.
   - Figure out how many degrees each part will represent (i.e., multiply each percentage by 360—the number of degrees in a circle). For example, multiply the percentage of books read in one month by 360.

More steps are on the back...

Appendix D: Resource Cards and Student Booklet Thumbnails

Resource Card — 91b

2. Draw the pie graph.
   - Use a compass (or a round object) and draw the size you desire for the chart.
   - Use a protractor to mark the number of degrees each part will represent on the graph.
   - Use the ruler to draw lines to the center of the circle.
   - Label each part of the graph so that the information is clear to the reader.

Pie Graph Example — Books Read by Class

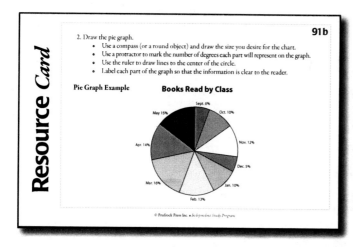

Resource Card — 92

Developing a Product—Poster

How do I make a poster?

Materials:
- poster board
- pencil/eraser
- ruler
- felt markers or crayons
- scratch paper
- pictures, drawings, etc.
- glue

Steps are on the back...

Resource Card — 92b

1. Plan the poster.
   - The poster should have a border around the outside; a title in large, bold letters; pictures or drawings; and labels or short written descriptions.
   - Decide how you want the poster to look and make a rough sketch on scratch paper. (Remember to keep it simple with only a few pictures, charts, and the like to label.)
   - On the poster board, make a border around the outside using the ruler and pencil. Measure from the outer edge 1–2 inches and mark it in several places around the entire poster. With a pencil, join the marks using the ruler as a straight edge. Put all pictures and drawings inside of the border.
   - Collect all of the information you want to include on the poster and lay it loosely on the poster, arranging it evenly. Make sure that you include room to put labels and written descriptions.
   - Decide how large the title letters should be and use the ruler and pencil to lightly draw straight lines as a guide.
2. Create the poster.
   - Draw the title letters in pencil or use large cut-out letters.
   - When they are spaced correctly, go over the penciled letters in ink or marker.
   - Glue the pictures or drawings to the poster board where you had them arranged.
   - Add the labels or written descriptions.
   - Either emphasize the border with an ink line or erase the pencil line.

Resource Card — 93

Developing a Product—PowerPoint Presentation

How do I create a PowerPoint presentation?

Materials:
- computer
- PowerPoint software on the computer
- pictures (digital) or graphics or pictures from the Internet

1. Plan the content.
   - Plan the information you want to present.
   - Use key words and phrases, not long sentences and paragraphs.
   - Decide what pictures you need. You may want to locate some on the Internet that are available for free use, or scan them, or insert them from a CD, DVD, or digital camera.
   - Include a title page and summary page.

More steps are on the back...

Resource Card — 93b

2. Create the PowerPoint slides.
   - Use the design templates provided by the program.
   - Type the main points of your study onto the slides, being careful not to use long sentences or paragraphs that are difficult to read.
   - Insert any pictures that enhance your presentation.
   - Add in special features, such as sound and animation, as necessary.
3. Practice your presentation in front of a friend.
   - Tell about the information as you present each slide. Speak clearly and don't read directly from the slide.
   - Ask your friend to tell you how you can improve your presentation. Make any changes necessary.

Tips for creating your PowerPoint Presentations:
- Use colors that go with the words. For example, if you are talking about the ocean, you might use a blue or blue-green background or font color to suggest the ocean. Avoid colors such as orange or red, as these are often difficult to read.
- Make the sound effects go with the topic. For example, if you are talking about the ocean, the sound of waves would be appropriate. You should avoid clapping hands or car-door slamming sound effects, because they will not enhance the meaning.
- Keep the words brief on each slide.
- Add pictures or graphics to slides for interest and understanding.

Resource Card — 94

Developing a Product—Puppet Show

How do I create a puppet show?

Materials
- materials will vary, depending on the kind of show
- index cards

1. Plan the puppet show.
   - Decide what topic, theme, or message you want to be the focus.
   - Write the ideas you want to include on index cards.
   - Sequence the cards. Order them by what you want to happen first, second, and so on.
   - Decide how many characters will be in the play and who will play each part. You may want to include a narrator (someone who tells what is happening in the story).
   - Using the note cards as guides, write the dialogue (what each character will say).
   - Decide how the play will be presented, what the stage will look like (behind a table covered with a sheet or in a large cardboard box, such as a refrigerator box, with a hole cut out for the puppets), and what props should be included in the set.
   - Plan what kind of puppets to use (paper sack, finger, pencil, papier mâché, rubber glove, etc.). See examples on the next card.

More steps are on the back...

Resource Card — 94b

2. Make the puppets and the stage.
3. Present the production.
   - If you have other students helping you present your show, practice reading the script with them before using the puppets.
   - Make sure that all players speak loudly and keep their faces turned toward the audience (even though they are out of sight).
   - Put the puppets in the order that they will appear in the show.
   - Practice reading the script using the puppets.
   - Time the show to see approximately how long it lasts.
   - Plan a time with the teacher to present the show to the class.

Resource Card — 95

Developing a Product—Puppet Show, Continued

Examples

Spoon Puppet — Finger Puppets — Paper Sack Puppet

Resource Card 96: Developing a Product—Report

How do I write a report?

Materials
- paper
- pencil or pen
- notes from topic studied
- computer (optional)

1. Plan and organize the report.
   - Look over the notes or outline you made when you were researching the topic.
   - Think about what you want to tell the audience. Most reports include the following items:
     - a statement of the question you are researching (what you studied);
     - discussion of the question (why you decided to study the question);
     - the method (how you studied the question);
     - the results (what you discovered in your study);
     - conclusions (what answers you found to the question);
     - bibliography (what resources, books, magazines, materials you used); and
     - acknowledgements (thanks to the people who helped you).

More steps are on the back...

© Prufrock Press Inc. • *Independent Study Program*

Resource Card 96b

- Write a rough draft, skipping every other line to leave room for corrections. It is not uncommon for great thinkers to write at least three rough drafts.
- Try to write the report using your own words. If you must use someone else's words, remember to use quotation marks and give credit to the source.
- Decide if you want to include pictures, drawings, graphs, or charts in the paper.
- Give the report a title.

2. Write the report.
   - Read the rough draft. Does it flow nicely from one idea to the next (transition)? Does it say what you want it to say? Does it sound like your work and not a rewriting of the sources you read?
   - Make the necessary additions and corrections in pencil.
   - In pen and on good paper, write the report in your best handwriting, or type your report on the computer.
   - Include a title page with the title of the report, the date the report is due, your name, your teacher's name, and the subject.

3. Proofread the report.
   - Does the report look neat?
   - Are all of the words spelled correctly (did you use spellchecker on the computer)?
   - Is it punctuated correctly?

© Prufrock Press Inc. • *Independent Study Program*

Resource Card 97: Developing a Product—Tape Recording

How do I make a tape recording?

Materials
- tape recorder
- blank cassette tape
- written script

1. Plan the script.
   - Decide what you want to tell the audience.
   - Write a script to guide you. Include exactly what you will say and what others will say, if you are including anyone else.
   - If you are recording an interview, you may write a list of possible questions you will ask the person. Tell the person before the interview the kinds of questions you will ask so he or she can prepare some answers.
   - Before you turn on the tape recorder, practice what you will say.

More steps are on the back...

© Prufrock Press Inc. • *Independent Study Program*

Resource Card 97b

2. Make the recording.
   - Try to record in a quiet area.
   - Keep the microphone steady and approximately 10–15 inches away from your mouth.
   - Watch the recording indicator to make sure that the sound level is correct. If the recorder does not have an indicator, check it by saying a few words into the recorder, rewind it, and then listen to the sound. Make necessary adjustments.
   - Give the title of what you are presenting, such as, "This is an interview with Dr. Young about color photography."
   - Speak clearly and slowly, but naturally.
   - If you want someone to do something, give an exact, short, clear instruction, such as "Turn to page 63 and read the first paragraph."
   - At the end of your recording, tell the listener to turn off the tape player and rewind the tape.

3. Evaluate the recording.
   - Have someone else listen to the tape to see if the information is clear and understandable.
   - Make any necessary changes.

© Prufrock Press Inc. • *Independent Study Program*

Resource Card 98: Developing a Product—Television Show

How do I make a television show?

Materials
- video recorder
- videotape or DVD
- props, as needed

1. Plan the TV Show.
   - Determine what you want the television show to be about. Do you want your TV show to be a sitcom, talk show, news broadcast, or something else?
   - Decide what props or costumes you need and collect them.
   - Write some notes of what you will say and in what order each part will happen.
   - If you have a time frame, try to judge how much time each segment will take.
   - Include an introduction and a wrap-up.

2. Videotape the show.
   - Set up the video camera on a tripod to keep it steady.
   - Assign someone to be the videographer who will do the filming.
   - Practice doing the show, and then videotape it as a dress rehearsal. The videographer may want to zoom in on some faces at certain points.

More steps are on the back...

© Prufrock Press Inc. • *Independent Study Program*

Resource Card 98b

3. Review the videotape and shoot the final version.
   - Replay the video dress rehearsal of the TV show and time it.
   - Discuss the strengths.
   - Discuss the parts that could be improved including poor or unclear dialogue and scenes that need revision. Rework those trouble spots.
   - Adjust the time, if needed. Do some parts need to move faster? Quicken the pace or eliminate some unnecessary words. Do some areas need more explanation? Add to it.
   - Videotape the final version.

Suggestions for Shows
- Think about some shows you like. Notice the features of a show and see how you might emulate it.
- Consider a news broadcast with breaking news about your topic of study. Bring on the experts to give information.
- You might want to do a point-counterpoint debate about an issue.
- Shows such as "Reading Rainbow" might demonstrate how to do book reviews and add a skit on the same topic.
- Add some creative drama by writing a script to a play.
- Talk shows can provide a wide range of subjects if several students combine their ideas to develop one video.

© Prufrock Press Inc. • *Independent Study Program*

Resource Card 99: Developing a Product—Timeline

What is a timeline?

A timeline is a graphic way to show a sequence of events.

How do I develop a timeline?

Materials
- poster board or paper
- makers or crayons
- pencil
- ruler
- pictures or drawings
- glue

Steps are on the back...

© Prufrock Press Inc. • *Independent Study Program*

Resource Card 99b

1. Plan the timeline.
   - Determine which years will be included on the timeline.
   - Decide whether the timeline will run horizontally or vertically.
   - Determine whether you will use pictures, drawings, special lettering, or any graphic design on the timeline.
   - Decide how long the timeline will be (this will determine the type of paper you will use for your timeline).
   - Figure out how long each time period will be. For example, ½ inch could equal one year, 5 years, 100 years, or any other time period you choose.

2. Draw the timeline.
   - Use a ruler and pencil to draw the timeline.
   - Divide the timeline into specific time periods.
   - In pencil, write the dates and information beside the timeline.
   - Place the pictures or drawings on the paper. When you are satisfied with the way they are arranged, glue them to the paper.
   - Write a title for the timeline. Use a pencil and rule to center the letters evenly. Go over all of the penciled letters in ink. Gently erase all pencil lines.

Note: If you would prefer to use your computer to make a timeline, use a search engine and enter "timeline." One Web site, http://www.teach-nology.com, allows you to enter the events and a timeline is created for you.

© Prufrock Press Inc. • *Independent Study Program*

Appendix D: Resource Cards and Student Booklet Thumbnails

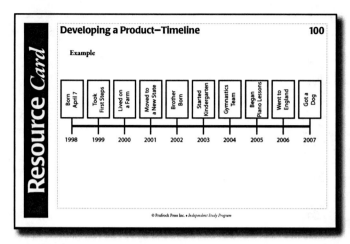

Resource Card

Developing a Product—Timeline — 100

Example

Timeline events (1998–2007): Born April 7; Took First Steps; Lived on a Farm; Moved to a New State; Brother Born; Started Kindergarten; Gymnastics Team; Began Piano Lessons; Went to England; Got a Dog.

© Prufrock Press Inc. • *Independent Study Program*

Resource Card

Developing a Product—Creating a Video — 101

How do I create a video?

Materials
- video camera
- videotape or DVD

1. Identify who is the intended audience for the video.
2. Identify the purpose of the video. Will you be presenting information about all of your research questions? Will you be teaching specific facts? Will you be teaching someone how to do something? Will you be demonstrating the results of an experiment?
3. Decide on the format and the location of the video. Will you be making a news broadcast? Will you be producing a play? Will you be describing something you created in your school? Outside your school?
4. Decide who is going to be in the video. Will you be the only person in the video? Will someone else be in the video? Who will help you videotape your production?

More steps are on the back…

© Prufrock Press Inc. • *Independent Study Program*

Resource Card — 101b

5. Write a script about what you and/or others will be saying in the video. Identify what props you may need to include.
6. Practice the script before you begin videotaping.
7. If you are going to be in the video, enlist your teacher or a friend to help with the taping.
8. When videotaping, remember these tips:
   - use a tripod to eliminate a jumpy video,
   - check for glare (do not aim your camera toward bright lights),
   - have a light background,
   - do a sound check,
   - cut off extraneous sounds, and
   - do a trial run to make sure that everything is working before you begin taping.
9. View the videotape to make sure that it works properly before sharing it with an audience.

© Prufrock Press Inc. • *Independent Study Program*

Resource Card

Developing a Product—Creating a Web Page — 102

How do I create a Web page?

Materials
- Computer with a software program that assists in the development of Web pages such as iWeb, Microsoft Word, and Microsoft FrontPage, among others.

1. Identify who is the intended audience for the Web page and what content you will include on the Web page. Remember to include your research questions.
2. Check out the school district's policies concerning the development of Web pages. What does the school say about using names, personal information about others, student pictures, and linking Web pages to the school?
3. Find out what authoring tools are available in your school (e.g., Microsoft FrontPage, Adobe Contribute, Macromedia Dreamweaver, Microsoft Word, iWeb).

More steps are on the back…

© Prufrock Press Inc. • *Independent Study Program*

Resource Card — 102b

4. Think about layout and design. What specific items will be included on the main page and linked pages? Remember to keep it simple. To help you think about designing a Web page, you will want to create a storyboard of ideas (see figure).

   As you design your Web page, think about including some or all of the items listed below.
   - Identification information, including author (use only your first name), document creation date, date of last revision, and links to the school or classroom's Web site (if permitted by school policy).
   - *Purpose of the page.* Stick to one purpose.
   - *Title of the page.*
   - *Your research questions.* Have each of your questions link to information about it.
   - *Inside links to pages of information that you have designed.* Remember to limit the number of clicks that visitors might need to use to access the information.
   - *Outside links to Internet information about your questions.* Make sure that the sites you include are reputable, reliable sources of information.

   (Storyboard diagram: Topic → Q1, Q2, Q3 → Facts, Photo, Link)

More steps are on the next Resource Card…

© Prufrock Press Inc. • *Independent Study Program*

Resource Card

Developing a Product—Creating a Web Page, Continued — 103

5. Use graphics sparingly because they take time to load. When using graphics, follow these guidelines:
   - keep them to a reasonable size. If they are larger than a 2-inch square or a 1 × 3 inch rectangle, use a thumbnail image of the picture.
   - keep the number of graphics on one page to a minimum and compress graphic files whenever possible.
   - reduce the color palette to the lowest possible palette size to ensure a quick download of your Web page.
   - graphics and clip art obtained from the Internet must be properly referenced.
   - when using photographs of students, be sure to obtain prior written permission by the students and their parents.
6. When using colors and fonts, remember these rules:
   - vary your font color. Light backgrounds should have dark text and dark backgrounds should have light text. It is important to remember, though, not to have too many colors on your Web site. Keep it simple and use only two or three colors.
   - vary your font size. Use larger font sizes for topics and smaller font sizes for subtopics, but remember that it is easier to read a Web site when there are only two or three different font sizes.

More steps are on the back…

© Prufrock Press Inc. • *Independent Study Program*

Resource Card — 103b

7. Plan how people will navigate within your Web site. Every page should have a link to the main menu page of the independent study (your research questions). If you have more than one page, you need to identify how the visitor will advance to the different pages and how they will return to the home page. You also need to decide how they will advance to the top or the page or to the bottom of the page.
8. Post the Web page.
9. Remember to update your Web page every 30 days to make it relevant to visitors.

© Prufrock Press Inc. • *Independent Study Program*

Resource Card

Presenting Information—Introduction — 104

Why do I present the product?

It is important to present the product because:
- others can learn from your information,
- you can get ideas from others about the product,
- you can improve the product,
- others can help evaluate the product, and
- you can gain the support of others.

Advertisers, artists, businesspersons, inventors, researchers, scientists, teachers, and other professionals always try to present products in the best possible manner.

© Prufrock Press Inc. • *Independent Study Program*

Resource Card 105: Presenting Information—Ways to Present

How do I present the information?

- *Oral report*—Sharing information with others in spoken form.
- *Demonstration*—A physical display that shows how something is done.
- *Performance*—An action that conveys information in an artistic manner.
- *Display*—A visual collection of information arranged for others to see in a visually appealing, interesting, or entertaining way.
- *Electronic display*—Information and graphics that are shown on a computer monitor or on another electronic device.

Resource Card 106: Presenting Information—Oral Report

How do I present an oral report?

1. Plan the report.
   - Find out how much time you have to present your report.
   - Decide what is the most important information you want your audience to learn.
   - Write the main ideas of the report on index cards.
   - Decide if you have other materials to show the class (posters, drawings, etc.).

2. Practice the presentation.
   - Use the index cards and practice the report out loud until you are comfortable with it.
   - Use a mirror, videotape yourself, or have someone listen to you.
   - Time the presentation to make sure that it is within the given time limits.

More steps are on the back...

Resource Card 106b

3. Present the report.
   - If you are showing materials, arrange them in the order you will show them.
   - Stand where everyone can see you and the materials you are presenting.
   - Introduce yourself if the audience does not know you and tell why you developed the product. Explain the study question(s) you asked in the beginning of the study.
   - Look at the audience when you speak. Do not read your report word-for-word or stare at your notes. Glance at them only as needed.
   - Speak loudly in order to be heard in the back of the room.
   - Hold your product high enough for everyone to see it. You may have someone else hold it while you discuss it.
   - State the major points about the product, but keep the talk short. (You don't want to bore the audience.)
   - When you have finished the presentation, ask if there are questions.
   - If you choose, have each person in the audience complete an evaluation form to give you information about what each thought about the product.
   - Thank the audience members for their attention.

Resource Card 107: Presenting Information—Demonstration

How do I demonstrate how to do something?

1. Plan the demonstration.
   - Determine where you will demonstrate how to do something and how much space you need.
   - Decide how this demonstration answers the study question(s).
   - Gather all of the materials and props you will require.
   - Make notes of how you will introduce the demonstration, what you will say during each step, and what you will say at the end.

2. Practice the demonstration.
   - Rehearse the demonstration until you are comfortable with it.
   - Time the demonstration to make sure it is within the allotted time frame.
   - Practice it in front of someone else and ask for feedback.
   - Work on the parts that need some improvement.

More steps are on the back...

Resource Card 107b

3. Present the demonstration.
   - Introduce yourself and tell the reasons why you chose to make this demonstration.
   - Explain how this demonstration connects to your study question(s).
   - Show the audience each of the steps.
   - Ask if the audience has any questions or comments.
   - If you choose, you might have a volunteer in the audience show what he or she has learned by demonstrating the steps to others.
   - Have the audience evaluate your performance.
   - Thank the audience for its attention.

Resource Card 108: Presenting Information—Performance

How do I present a performance?

1. Plan the performance.
   - Determine where you will perform and how much space you need.
   - Decide how this performance answers the study question(s).
   - Gather all of the materials and props you will require.
   - Make notes of how you will introduce the performance and what you will say at the end.

2. Practice the performance.
   - Rehearse the performance until you are comfortable with it.
   - Time the performance to make sure it is within the allotted time frame.
   - Practice it in front of someone else and ask for feedback.
   - Work on the parts that need some improvement.

More steps are on the back...

Resource Card 108b

3. Present the performance.
   - Introduce yourself and tell why you are presenting this performance. Explain how this performance connects to your study question(s).
   - Perform.
   - Ask if the audience has any questions or comments.
   - If you choose, have the audience members evaluate your performance.
   - Thank the audience members for their attention.

Resource Card 109: Presenting Information—Display

How do I present a display?

1. Plan the display.
   - Determine how much space is available for the display.
   - Decide what the display should look like (see examples on next card).
   - Gather all materials necessary to make the display.
   - Write a few notes on index cards to remind yourself of points you want to include in the presentation.

2. Make the display.
   - Use colorful, cutout letters for the title of the display, if possible. (Your teacher may have some stencils or letters you can use.)
   - Include drawings, diagrams, pictures, and other items that will help to explain the study.

3. Present the display.
   - Use your notes to discuss the display in an orderly manner.
   - Invite the audience members to look closely at the display after the presentation.
   - Answer questions from audience members about the display.

Examples are on the next Resource Card...

Appendix D: Resource Cards and Student Booklet Thumbnails

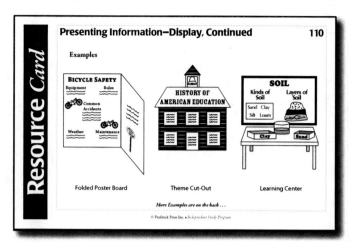

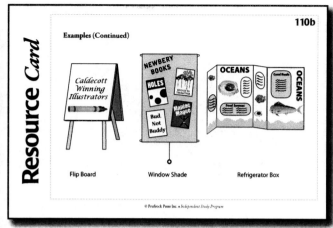

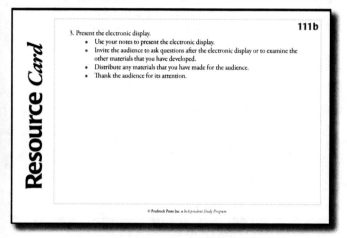

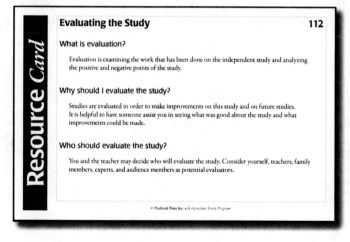

Chapter 1
Introduction: Beginning My Independent Study

With your teacher and classmates, or by yourself, write down what you think "independent study" might mean.

_____
_____
_____
_____
_____
_____

Write below what the independent study process will mean to you as you begin your study.

_____
_____
_____
_____
_____
_____
_____

Planning My Study

As you move through your independent study, check (✔) the steps you use. Only some of these steps will apply to your study.

____ Selecting a Topic	Due Date _____
❑ Subtopic of a class unit	❑ Something I was curious about
❑ Something I wanted to learn more about	❑ Something I know a lot about

____ Organizing a Topic	Due Date _____
❑ Description	❑ Causes and Effects
❑ Comparison	❑ Problems and Solutions

____ Asking Questions	Due Date _____
❑ Used stem words	❑ Wrote Little Thinking Questions
❑ Wrote More Thinking Questions	❑ Wrote Most Thinking Questions

____ Using a Study Method	Due Date _____		
❑ Descriptive	❑ Historical	❑ Developmental	❑ Case Study
❑ Correlation	❑ Action	❑ Experimental	❑ Factual Information

____ Collecting Information   Due Date _____

Information Sources:
- ❑ Internet   ❑ Electronic   ❑ Places
- ❑ People   ❑ Print/Text

Ways to Collect:
- ❑ Interview   ❑ Experiment   ❑ Observation
- ❑ Reading   ❑ Correspondence

____ Developing a Product	Due Date _____
❑ Reviewed various products	❑ Developed a plan
❑ Product created _____	

____ Presenting Information	Due Date _____
❑ Oral Report	❑ Demonstration
❑ Performance Display	❑ Electronic Display

____ Evaluating the Study	Due Date _____
❑ Self	❑ Teacher ❑ Audience

Checklist for Guiding Independent Studies

Check (✔) your response to each question as you go through each step of the study.

	Student Response	
	Yes	No
Selecting a Topic		
• Did I choose a topic I'm interested in learning about?	___	___
• Do I have enough time to study this topic?	___	___
Organizing a Topic		
• Did I use stem words to think of questions about my topic?	___	___
• Did I choose a More or Most Thinking question to study?	___	___
Using a Study Method		
• Did I choose a study method?	___	___
• Did I use the study method to help my thinking about the topic?	___	___
Collecting Information		
• Did I use several resources to find information?	___	___
• Did I take notes and cite my sources?	___	___
Developing a Product		
• Did I plan a way to showcase my information?	___	___
• Did I use my time well to create my product?	___	___
Presenting Information		
• Did I practice my presentation and make improvements?	___	___
• Did I share my new learning with an audience?	___	___
Evaluating the Study		
• Did I analyze the strengths and weaknesses of my study?	___	___
• Did I notice how to improve future studies?	___	___

Conference Planning Guide

When you are ready to talk with your teacher, complete this sheet in preparation. You may confer several times.

Independent Study Topic _____

Circle type of conference:
- Selecting a Topic
- Organizing a Topic
- Asking Questions
- Using a Study Method
- Collecting Information
- Developing a Product
- Presenting Information
- Evaluating the Study

During the conference, I want to focus on:

_____
_____
_____
_____
_____
_____
_____
_____
_____
_____

Appendix D: Resource Cards and Student Booklet Thumbnails

Chapter 2
Selecting My Topic

If you are selecting a topic on your own, complete these two pages. If you are doing an independent study on a topic the whole class is studying, skip these two pages and go to the next section, titled Subtopics.

Who are some well-known people I'm curious about?

_____
_____
_____
_____

If I selected a nonfiction book to read today, what subjects would interest me?

_____
_____
_____
_____
_____

Independent Study Program Student Booklet © Prufrock Press Inc.

Selecting My Topic

Some hobbies I enjoy or would like to try are:

_____
_____
_____
_____
_____

A country or place I would like to visit one day is _____. Why?

_____
_____
_____
_____

After reading over the topic ideas on the Resource Cards, these were the most intriguing to me:

_____
_____
_____
_____
_____

Independent Study Program Student Booklet © Prufrock Press Inc.

Selecting My Topic—Finding Subtopics

If you will do an independent study project on a subject you are already studying in school, complete this page.

What is the big topic you are studying?

_____

List as many smaller subtopics about this big topic as you can think of:

_____
_____
_____
_____
_____
_____
_____
_____
_____
_____

Circle three of the subtopics that you might like to learn more about.

Independent Study Program Student Booklet © Prufrock Press Inc.

Selecting My Topic—Evaluating the Topics

Sometimes it's hard to make a choice about the best topic to study. Evaluating with a grid is one way to help you choose. Study this example.

Reasons for Selecting a Topic for Research

- It is the most interesting topic to me.
- It is the most useful.
- It has the most information written about it.
- Information would be easy to find.
- I know a lot about this topic already and want to learn more.
- Other reasons: _____

Example of an Evaluation Grid

Topics	Most interesting topic	Most useful topic	Information easy to find	Total
1. advertising	1	3	1	5
2. photography	5	4	2	11
3. wolves	4	1	3	8
4. pollution	2	5	4	11
5. Chris Van Allsburg	3	2	5	10

Based on this Evaluation Grid, which topic should I study? Both photography and pollution got the same score. When I considered both topics, I decided to go with photography because it was the most interesting to me. The final decision was mine and now I'm ready to go!

Independent Study Program Student Booklet © Prufrock Press Inc.

Selecting My Topic—Evaluating My Topics

Directions for Evaluating My Topics

1. Select several topics to judge. Write these on the lines of the grid on the next page.
2. Think of some reasons why you might study these topics. Write these reasons in the vertical spaces at the top of the grid.
3. Now rank each topic from 1 (least favorite) to however many topics you listed, with the highest number being the favorite.
4. Add the numbers across on each row and put the total in the right-hand box.
5. The highest number should be the best topic for you to study.
6. If there is a tie, you decide which of those topics is most interesting to you to study.

Possible Reasons for Selecting a Topic for Research

- It is the most interesting topic to me.
- I am curious about this topic.
- It is the most useful.
- It has the most information written about it.
- Information would be easy to find.
- I know a lot about this topic already and want to learn more.
- It is often in the news and is a current topic.
- Several friends are studying this topic and we could work together.
- Other reasons: _____

Selecting My Topic—Evaluation Grid

	Reasons				Total
Topics					
1.					
2.					
3.					
4.					
5.					

Chapter 3
Organizing My Topic

Answer the questions below to help you think about organizing your topic.

When you organize your desk, what do you do?
_____
_____
_____

How do you think you might organize a clothes closet?
_____
_____
_____

How do you think you might organize a topic?
_____
_____
_____

These are four different ways to organize a topic:

- *Description*—tell about your topic in one or more ways
- *Comparison*—compare your topic to something else
- *Causes and Effects*—identify possible causes and effects that have influenced the topic
- *Problems and Solutions*—describe problems and solutions that relate to the topic

Organizing My Topic by Description

How might I organize my topic by description?

Description is a way you can explain or tell more about your topic. You might want to describe your topic in one or more of the following ways:

• its different parts	• its contributions
• feelings about it	• how it is measured
• criticisms about it	• its future
• its different features	• its different uses
• beliefs about it	• its family
• how it works	• different types
• different kinds	• where it lives
• its history	• how it grows
• how it has changed	• how it is built
• its stages	• its habits

Appendix D: Resource Cards and Student Booklet Thumbnails

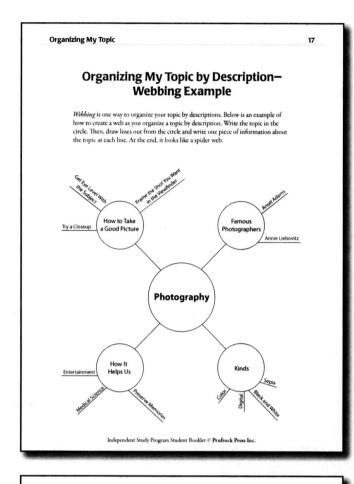

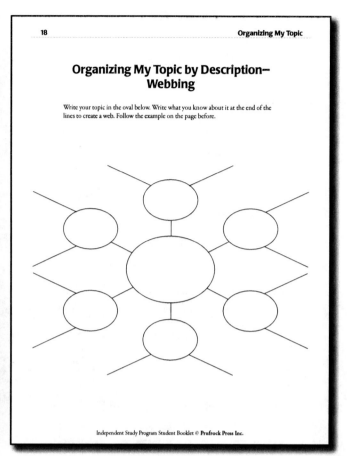

Organizing My Topic by Comparison

How might I organize my topic by comparison?

When you *compare* two things, you look at how they are alike and different. There are several ways to compare your topic to another topic, a perfect model, or a rule. You might compare your topic with something else by looking at:
- how they look
- how they are used
- their histories
- their futures
- how people feel about them
- how they grow and change

Example:

Ways of Comparison	My Topic: Amphibians	Comparison: Reptiles
Appearance	Smooth skin or thick, leathery skin	Dry, scaly skin
Home	Lives on land near water and underground	Hole, under rocks, or in the ocean
Defense	Protective coloring and staying out of sight, and poison	Protective coloring, plays tricks, and strength
Food	Plants, small animals, and insects	Animals and plants
Growth	Metamorphosis	Shed skin
Communication	Sensing or calls	Sense vibrations

Organizing My Topic by Comparison

If you think you might organize your topic by comparing it to something else, write your ideas here.

Ways of Comparison	My Topic:	Comparison:

Organizing My Topic by Causes and Effects

How might I organize my topic by causes and effects?

Identify how the topic has changed or may change. Decide which of the changes you might want to study:
- from the past to the present
- from the present to the future
- its parts or structure
- its usefulness
- its beliefs or beliefs about it
- its purpose
- its habits

You examine the things that always seem to happen before the change (that is the cause) and the things that always seem to happen after the change (that is the effect).

Things that have changed:

_____
_____
_____

Example

Topic: Communities: How They Developed

Causes	Change	Effects
Early humans located in climates where they could survive more easily.	Humans moved from place to place.	Organized culture—religion; communication and transportation systems; gender and age roles; the arts; and so on.
Early humans needed to locate near a food source.	Humans formed villages and began to farm land, living near water sources.	Technological advances such as domesticating plants and animals and eventually the industrial revolution.
Early humans needed to secure a dependable supply of food.		
When early humans worked together, they were better able to survive.		Urban, suburban, and rural societies.

Organizing My Topic by Causes and Effects

If you would like to study more about your topic's causes and effects, then complete the chart below.

Topic: _____

Causes	Change	Effects

Organizing My Topic by Problems and Solutions

How might I organize my topic by problems and solutions?

When you *organize a topic by problems and solutions*, you explore a difficult situation, question, or puzzle and think of possible ways to solve the problem. To identify difficulties (problems) in which more than one solution is possible, you can look at:
- a difference between what is wanted and what is happening now,
- a difference between what is happening now and what might happen in the future,
- a difference between what is really happening and what is only imagined to be happening, and
- what might happen in the future if a change does or doesn't happen.

When you have identified a problem, you can explore possible solutions in one or more of the following ways:

S	*substitute* a new part for an old part (e.g., Velcro shoe fasteners for laces)
C	*combine* two good ideas to make a new idea (e.g., wheels on backpacks)
A	*adapt* an idea from somewhere else (e.g., drive-through grocery store)
M	*modify* the meaning, magnify (make it bigger), or minimize (make it smaller; e.g., small laptop computers)
P	*put to other uses* or use it in other places (e.g., use cans to create art objects)
E	*eliminate* something, make it smaller, lower, or shorter (e.g., pocket-size digital cameras)
R	*rearrange* the order of things (e.g., place desserts in the front of a cafeteria line)

Chapter 4
Asking Questions

What is an effective study question?

An Effective Study Question:
- encourages more than one possible answer.
- requires plenty of time to study it.
- has resources available to gather information about it.
- is useful or beneficial.

Which are good study questions?

Write an "E" or an "I" in front of each question to tell if it is an effective or an ineffective study question.

_____ 1. Who were the characters in Huckleberry Finn?
_____ 2. Do students who get A's in school study more than students who get B's?
_____ 3. Which living creatures are in danger of becoming extinct?
_____ 4. How many different kinds of whales are there?
_____ 5. How do children in different cultures learn to talk?
_____ 6. What were the most important changes in my school in the last 5 years?
_____ 7. How is pollution controlled in different parts of the world?
_____ 8. What kinds of equipment are used at a weather station?
_____ 9. What does my teacher think about recycling paper products?

Transform one of the ineffective study questions into an effective question.

_____
_____

Answers: 1. I, 2. E, 3. E, 4. I, 5. E, 6. E, 7. E, 8. I, 9. I

Appendix D: Resource Cards and Student Booklet Thumbnails

Asking Questions — 25

Asking Questions—Using Stem Words

Stem words (sometimes known as the "W" and "H" words) can help you think of questions. Write some questions about your topic that begin with these words.

WHO	
WHAT	
WHEN	
WHERE	
WHY	
HOW	

Independent Study Program Student Booklet © Prufrock Press Inc.

---

26 — **Asking Questions**

Asking Questions—Asking Higher Level Thinking Questions

What are the kinds of questions you can ask?

> There are three levels of questions you can ask:
> 1. Questions that require *little* thinking,
> 2. Questions that require *more* thinking, and
> 3. Questions that require the *most* thinking.

Little Thinking Questions

Little Thinking Questions are those that can be answered by using known information. You can find the answers by simply copying or redoing something that someone else has done. These types of questions need to be answered when you are building a foundation of knowledge or first learning about your topic. For example:

Q: What are the different kinds of hummingbirds?
To answer this question, you might summarize information from a bird book.

More Thinking Questions

More Thinking Questions are those that can be answered when you use information you already know in new situations. These types of questions may be answered after you already know something about your topic. For example:

Q: How might birds that have become extinct survive in our communities today?
To answer this question, you would need to identify some birds that have become extinct, learn about their habitats and why they became extinct, and then identify if the community's habitat would support them today.

Most Thinking Questions

Most Thinking Questions are those that can be answered when you create and/or evaluate new information. These types of questions are answered by new inventions, creations, or discoveries that require a lot of knowledge about your topic. For example:

Q: How might you develop a way to protect birds in cities?
To answer this question, you could develop a plan to present to the city council.

Q: Which plan do you think will be most effective in protecting birds?
To answer this question, you could establish criteria and evaluate each of the proposed plans.

Independent Study Program Student Booklet © Prufrock Press Inc.

Asking Questions — 27

Asking Questions—Little, More, or Most Thinking?

1. On the lines below, write the words *little*, *more*, or *most* to indicate the level of thinking.
2. Underneath, write the types of information you might need to collect.

> **Example**
>
> *more*   What might be the future effects of the destruction of rain forests?
> *Information about rain forests, how they contribute to the world; analyze effects on people, places, and things if they were gone (new situation)*

_____ 1. How might we protect animals that are endangered?
_____

_____ 2. How has communication changed in the past 30 years? Given these changes, in what ways might we communicate in the future?
_____

_____ 3. How might you plan a family reunion?
_____

_____ 4. Who were the first five presidents of the United States?
_____

_____ 5. Who do you think is the best writer in class? Why?
_____

_____ 6. What improvements might you make on computers to increase their speed?
_____

_____ 7. How many people in my class like rap music?
_____

Answers: 1. most, 2. more, 3. most, 4. little, 5. most, 6. most, 7. little, 8. more

Independent Study Program Student Booklet © Prufrock Press Inc.

---

28 — **Asking Questions**

Asking Questions—Raising the Level of Questions

Read the Little Thinking Question and then rewrite it into a More Thinking or Most Thinking Question.

Little Thinking Question	More Thinking or Most Thinking Question
Example What are the four kinds of wolves?	In what ways might we prevent wolves from becoming endangered species?
Do you like to read?	
What is the smallest state in the United States?	
Where are rain forests located?	
How many bones are in the human body?	

Independent Study Program Student Booklet © Prufrock Press Inc.

Asking Questions—Writing Study Questions

Write some study questions about your topic. If you are having difficulty writing some More Thinking or Most Thinking Questions, you may need to read more about your topic first.

Little Thinking Questions	
More Thinking Questions	
Most Thinking Questions	

Asking Questions—Identifying Questions for Study

Review the study questions you wrote on the previous pages. Think about some criteria for judging effective study questions, then choose your best questions and list them below.

- Which questions do I have resources for?
- Which questions might I answer within the time that I have?
- Which questions are the most interesting to me?
- Which questions are most beneficial?
- Which questions require the most thinking?
- Other: _____

Chapter 5
Using a Study Method

What is a study method?

A study method describes certain steps that you will follow when you study your questions.

Check the study method below that is the best way to answer the questions of your study. It may be helpful for you to look at Resource Cards 20–38 in the Study Method section to see examples of each method.

- ☐ 1. *Factual Study*—The answer to the question will require collecting facts.
- ☐ 2. *Descriptive Study*—The answer to the question will require describing something with numbers or facts.
- ☐ 3. *Historical Study*—The answer to the question will require analyzing the past or history of my topic.
- ☐ 4. *Developmental Study*—The answer to the question will require observing the development of or changes in my topic.
- ☐ 5. *Case Study*—The answer to the question will require observing closely a person, animal, group, system, or thing.
- ☐ 6. *Correlation Study*—The answer to the question will require relating one thing with another thing using numbers.
- ☐ 7. *Action Study*—The answer to the question will require examining an improvement that is made to solve a problem.
- ☐ 8. *Experimental Study*—The answer to the question will require conducting an experiment and looking carefully at the results.

Using a Study Method—Matching the Method to the Study Questions

Draw lines from each study question to the method that matches it best.

1. Factual Study   A. How has our town changed since I was born?
2. Descriptive Study   B. What does the principal in my school do during one day?
3. Historical Study   C. How quickly do crayons melt when the temperature is 100 degrees?
4. Developmental Study   D. How are heights of people related to how fast they run?
5. Case Study   E. What do green herons look like?
6. Correlation Study   F. How many minutes do my classmates spend playing video games?
7. Action Study   G. How do tadpoles grow into frogs?
8. Experimental Study   H. How might I get more people to recycle trash in my school?

Answers: 1. E, 2. F, 3. A, 4. G, 5. B, 6. D, 7. H, 8. C

Appendix D: Resource Cards and Student Booklet Thumbnails

Page 33 — Using a Study Method

Using a Study Method—Identifying the Method and the Steps for Your Study

Review the different study methods. Think about which one you will use for your study. Using the steps identified in the Resource Cards, indicate below what you will do first, second, third, and so on to gather information for your study. You will want to identify specific sources and types of information, tests, definitions of variables, and/or participants.

_____

Independent Study Program Student Booklet © Prufrock Press Inc.

Page 34

Chapter 6
Collecting Information

Where can I find information?

Almost all the information you will find will come from varied sources such as:
- the Internet
- electronic sources
- objects for experiments
- people
- places
- print/text

Write which resources you think may be useful for answering your questions. Beside them, write more specifically who, what, or where.

Example

Q: What are the habits of cheetahs?
I can find information at the local zoo and from someone at the Zoological Society.

Independent Study Program Student Booklet © Prufrock Press Inc.

Page 35 — Collecting Information

Collecting Information—Using Varied Methods

In what ways can I collect information?

- conducting an experiment
- corresponding by letter or e-mail
- interviewing
- observing
- reading
- searching the Internet
- conducting a survey

Write on the lines below the several ways that you will collect information from your sources to answer your questions. Beside them, write more specifically the information that you hope to gather.

Example

Q: What are the habits of cheetahs?
I can collect information by interviewing—I will talk to the zookeeper about the habits of cheetahs.

Independent Study Program Student Booklet © Prufrock Press Inc.

Page 36 — Collecting Information

Collecting Information—Organizing Information

Check the ways that you will organize your information.

- ☐ classifying
- ☐ outlining
- ☐ summarizing
- ☐ taking notes
- ☐ using index cards
- ☐ webbing

Describe in more detail how you will organize your information. Will you use note cards? Folders? A journal? A particular computer program? Will you color code information? Organize it by your questions? Organize it by sources? Organize it by dates?

Example

I will organize my information using folders. I will label each of my folders with a specific question. I will print or copy each thing that I read and place it behind the question that it will answer. Within the folder, I will group these things by topic and subtopic. For example, my folder will be labeled, "What are the habits of cheetahs?" Within the folder, I will use color tabs to indicate if the article is talking primarily about where they live or how they relate to other animals.

Independent Study Program Student Booklet © Prufrock Press Inc.

Chapter 7
Developing a Product

What is a product?

> A product is something that is created or performed to give information to others about the questions you have studied.

Answer the questions below.

1. What information from your questions do you need to share?

   _____
   _____
   _____

2. Who might be interested in learning more about the answers to your questions?

   _____
   _____
   _____

3. Review some possible products from the Resource Cards that you think might showcase your information best and list them below:

   _____
   _____
   _____

Developing a Product—Choosing the Best Product to Showcase My Information

Products	Reasons			Total
1.				
2.				
3.				
4.				
5.				

Developing My Product— Visualizing My Product

Draw a sketch of what you think your final product might look like.

Developing My Product—Making My Product Plan

What is a product plan?

> A product plan is a system used in planning and developing the product.

The plan should include:
- a list of steps to follow to complete the product,
- all materials needed to develop the product, and
- a specific amount of time needed for each step.

Complete the chart below, filling in the steps you need to follow in order to develop your product.

What Materials Will I Need?	Where Can I Get Them?
What Steps Should I Follow?	**How Much Time Will This Take?**

Appendix D: Resource Cards and Student Booklet Thumbnails

41

Chapter 8
Presenting Information

Why should I present my findings?

I present my information so that:
- others can learn from my information,
- I can get ideas from others about the product,
- I can improve the product,
- others can help evaluate the product, and
- I can gain the support of others.

What are some ways I might present my information?

Check the way that you think will present your information best.

- ☐ *oral report*—presentation that involves talking to the audience and telling them about the information that was learned
- ☐ *demonstration*—physical display given to others about how something is done or how something works.
- ☐ *performance*—presentation of an artistic work, such as a play, dance, creative drama, or piece of music.
- ☐ *display*—presentation that often shows pictures, graphs, or charts, and brief bulleted points of information that are clearly visible. These include:
  - poster board or foam board;
  - tri-fold display board;
  - cardboard shape (shaped in the topic of the report);
  - refrigerator box;
  - chart paper;
  - window shade pull-down;
  - large cardboard box (use all four sides plus the top to show information)
- ☐ *electronic display*—display that showcases information using electronic forms such as computer programs, videos, DVD/CDs, and audiotapes.

You can also do a combination of two or more of these if you choose.

Independent Study Program Student Booklet © Prufrock Press Inc.

---

42   Presenting Information

Presenting Information–Presentation Checklist

> *The final performance which may take a minute has been preceded by many hours of rehearsal.*
> —L. P. Smith

How do I present information?

After you have practiced your presentation, read the questions and check "yes" or "no" for each. For any question with a "no" response, see how you can work on that part to make it a "yes." Now, you're ready to present!

	Yes	No
1. Have I prepared the materials (handouts, overhead transparencies, display, etc.) needed in my presentation?		
2. Have I practiced my presentation out loud (in front of a mirror or in front of another person)?		
3. Have I timed my talk?		
4. Have I made brief notes on index cards of the main ideas I will discuss?		
5. When I practiced my presentation, did I . . .		
• speak loudly enough for the audience to hear?		
• tell the topic and study question?		
• glance at my notes only when I needed them?		
• show the display or materials smoothly along with my talk?		
• ask if there were any questions?		
• thank the audience for listening?		

Independent Study Program Student Booklet © Prufrock Press Inc.

43

Chapter 9
Evaluating My Independent Study

What is evaluation?

> Evaluation is examining the work that has been done during the independent study and analyzing the strengths and weaknesses of the study.

Why should I evaluate my study?

Studies are evaluated in order to make improvements on the study and on future studies.

On the lines below, write why you think it is important to evaluate your study.

_____
_____
_____

Who evaluates the studies?

Several people often evaluate independent studies. These are usually people who have been involved in the study or who have listened to your presentation.

On the lines below, write who will evaluate your study:

_____
_____
_____

Independent Study Program Student Booklet © Prufrock Press Inc.

---

44   Evaluating My Independent Study

Evaluating My Independent Study–Self-Evaluation

Name_____ Date_____

Topic_____

Circle the number beside the statement that most accurately represents your thoughts about the quality of your product, the product's relationship to your topic, and the process that you used during your independent study:

	Disagree				Agree
I wrote probing study questions.	1	2	3	4	5
I developed a product that related to my questions.	1	2	3	4	5
I used a study method that related to my questions.	1	2	3	4	5
I collected information from more than one source.	1	2	3	4	5
The product I developed related to my research.	1	2	3	4	5
My product showed that I understood the important concepts of the topics.	1	2	3	4	5
I considered the audience when I made my presentation.	1	2	3	4	5
The product was attractive, professional, and interesting to the audience.	1	2	3	4	5
The product was original—something I had never done before.	1	2	3	4	5
The product was advanced beyond my grade level.	1	2	3	4	5
Throughout the study, I used my time efficiently and followed my plan.	1	2	3	4	5

What I did well:

_____
_____

The most difficult part was:

_____
_____

What I would change:

_____
_____

New questions I would ask about my topic:

_____
_____

Independent Study Program Student Booklet © Prufrock Press Inc.

Evaluating My Independent Study— Teacher Evaluation

Name_____ Date_____

Topic_____

Circle the number beside each statement that most accurately represents your thoughts about the quality of the student's product, the product's relationship to the student's topic, and the process that the student used during the independent study:

	Disagree				Agree
The student wrote probing study questions.	1	2	3	4	5
The student developed a product that related to the questions.	1	2	3	4	5
The student used a study method that related to the questions.	1	2	3	4	5
The student collected information from more than one source.	1	2	3	4	5
The product the student developed related to the research.	1	2	3	4	5
The student's product showed that the student understood the important concepts of the topics.	1	2	3	4	5
The student considered the audience when he or she made the presentation.	1	2	3	4	5
The product was attractive, professional, and interesting to the audience.	1	2	3	4	5
The product was original—something the student had never done before.	1	2	3	4	5
The product was advanced beyond the student's grade level.	1	2	3	4	5
Throughout the study, the student used time efficiently and followed a plan.	1	2	3	4	5

What the student did well:
_____
_____

The most difficult part for the student was:
_____
_____

Areas that need improving:
_____
_____

Independent Study Program Student Booklet © Prufrock Press Inc.

Evaluating My Independent Study— Audience Evaluation

Presenter(s)_____ Date_____

Topic_____

Check the box next to each statement that most accurately represents your thoughts about the quality of the student's product and presentation:

The presenter:	Yes	Not Sure	No
spoke clearly	☐	☐	☐
looked at the audience	☐	☐	☐
described the study questions	☐	☐	☐
answered the study questions	☐	☐	☐
made the information understandable	☐	☐	☐
made the information interesting	☐	☐	☐

I learned:
_____
_____

The most interesting part of the presentation was:
_____
_____

Questions I have about the study:
_____
_____

During the presentation I:
- ☐ listened
- ☐ discussed
- ☐ read something
- ☐ asked questions
- ☐ answered questions
- ☐ made something

Independent Study Program Student Booklet © Prufrock Press Inc.

Glossary

anecdotal record—a written account of observations about a person or event, particularly about how a student is learning, using strategies, and working through the independent study process.

audience—the people who are watching and listening to students present the information they have learned through their independent studies.

average—a number that can be regarded as typical of a group of numbers, calculated by adding the numbers together, then dividing the total by the amount of numbers; the level, amount, or degree of something that is typical of a group of things.

bias—an unfair preference for or dislike of something; the distortion of a set of statistical results by a variable not considered in the calculation.

brainstorm—the process of generating creative ideas spontaneously in an intensive group discussion that does not allow time for reflection.

categorize—to place something in a particular group.

causes and effects—a way to organize a topic that looks at the reasons that something happens and the changes that occur as a result of an action.

classify—to assign things to classes or groups.

correlation—a relationship between two or more things.

criteria—an accepted standard used in making decisions or judgments about something.

demonstration—a physical display that shows how something is done.

details—specific facts about something or somebody.

diagram—a simple drawing, chart, or graph that illustrates how something looks, changes, or works.

diorama—a three-dimensional representation of a scene.

direct observation—careful observation and recording about something that is happening, particularly how a child is learning.

display—visual presentations that often show pictures, graphs, or charts, and brief bulleted points of information.

evaluation—a spoken or written statement of the quality of an independent study.

electronic display—a visual showing of information on a computer or other electronic device.

generalization—a statement or conclusion that is derived from and applies equally to a number of cases.

graph—a diagram used to indicate relationships between two or more variable quantities. The quantities are measured along two axes, usually at right angles.

independent study—the self-directed process one uses when researching a new topic by him- or herself or with others.

interview—a meeting during which somebody is asked questions by a researcher.

little thinking questions—questions that can be answered by using information that is known.

main idea—the most important thought or concept.

mode—the numeral or value that has the highest frequency within a statistical range.

more thinking questions—questions that can be answered when you use information you already know in new situations.

most thinking questions—questions that can be answered when you create and/or evaluate new information.

unbiased sample—a random selection of individuals who represent perspectives of a larger group of individuals.

noticing special features strategy—the teacher guides students to pay attention to the important characteristics of professional products.

oral report—a verbal telling of information to others.

outline—a list of the main points of a subject that is being studied.

paired learning—a strategy in which two students work together to present information, listen to, give feedback to, and support each other throughout independent studies.

performance—an action that conveys information in an artistic manner.

product—a way to show what has been learned; something that students create that reflects the information learned throughout the study.

product plan—an organization tool that helps students plan the steps and estimated time for developing their products.

questionnaire—a set of questions used to gather information in a survey.

random sample—selecting participants in such a way that all have an equal chance of being included.

Glossary

range—the distance between the highest and lowest scores, ages, or variables being studied.

rating scale—measuring the quality, quantity, or frequency of a particular characteristic or variable.

reliability—the consistency or stability of scores or observations.

report—to give detailed information about a research topic or an investigation.

research—a methodical investigation into a subject in order to discover facts and gain knowledge or to develop a plan of action based on the facts discovered; to investigate, study, explore, delve into, or seek answers.

Resource Cards—a set of individual 5 ½" × 8 ½" cards in the *Independent Study Program* that students and teachers may refer to for assistance and ideas, additional information, and examples for each step of the research process.

rubric—a set of informational points that guide how students will be assessed.

salutation—the part of a letter that greets or addresses the recipient, such as "Dear Sir or Madam" or "Dear Ms. Anderson."

sampling error—the degree to which the selected sample is different from the entire population.

scaffolding—the support that teachers give students as they build new skills and strategies. Teachers model, engage, teach, and guide as they gradually move students toward independent learning.

self-assessment—thinking carefully about one's own strengths and areas to improve.

skim—to read something quickly, looking only for the general idea of the content.

steps of an independent study—the steps followed in the *Independent Study Program*, including Selecting a Topic, Organizing a Topic, Asking Questions, Using a Study Method, Collecting Information, Developing a Product, Presenting Information, and Evaluating the Study.

study method—a set of steps that students might follow to study a question; the *Independent Study Program* presents eight methods, including factual study, descriptive study, historical study, developmental study, case study, correlation study, action study, and experimental study.

study questions—questions asked for information about a topic.

subtopic—smaller components of a general subject being studied.

summarize—to give a shortened version of information that students have studied, stating only the main points.

survey—an analysis of answers to a poll of a sample of a population to determine opinions or knowledge about a specific question.

taking notes—a shortened way of writing information that is written or heard.

tape recording—using an electronic device to document what is heard.

think-aloud strategy—a technique teachers use to demonstrate how they think through a process by talking about their thoughts in a step-by-step manner.

timeline—a linear representation of significant events about a subject that are shown in chronological order.

topic—a subject written or spoken about.

validity—when the assessment brings about the results it is supposed to do.

visualization strategy—a technique students use to create vivid mental pictures of something, such as a desired outcome to a problem.

"W" and "H" questions—questions that begin with "W" and "H," such as who, what, when, where, why, and how.

References

Anderson, L. W., Krathwohl, D. R., Airasian, P. W., Cruikshank, K. A., Mayer, R. E., Pintrich, P. R., et al. (Eds.). (2001). *A taxonomy for learning, teaching and assessing: A revision of Bloom's taxonomy of educational objectives.* New York: Longman.

Atkin, J. M., Black, P., Coffey, J. (Eds.). (2001). *Classroom assessment and the national science education standards.* Washington, DC: National Academy Press.

Betts, G. T. (1985). *The autonomous learner model for gifted and talented.* Greeley, CO: ALPS.

Clark, B. (2002). *Growing up gifted: Developing the potential of children at home and at school* (6th ed.). Upper Saddle River, NJ: Prentice Hall.

Colangelo, N., & Davis, G. A. (Eds.). (2003). *Handbook of gifted education* (3rd ed.). Needham Heights, MA: Allyn & Bacon.

Coleman, L. J., & Cross, R. L. (2005). *Being gifted in school* (2nd ed.). Waco, TX: Prufrock Press.

Davis, G. A., & Rimm, S. B. (1998). *Education of the gifted and talented* (4th ed.). Needham Heights, MA: Allyn & Bacon.

Darling-Hammond, L., Ancess, J., & Falk, B. (1995). *Authentic assessment in action: Studies of schools and students at work.* New York: Teachers College Press.

Dunn, R., & Griggs, S. (1985). Teaching and counseling gifted students with their learning style preferences: Two case studies. *G/C/T, 14,* 40–43.

Eberle, B. (1996). *Scamper: Creative games and activities for imagination and development.* Buffalo, NY: D. O. K.

Encyclopedia Britannica Online. (n.d.). *Scaffold.* Retrieved May 2, 2007, from http://www.britannica.com/eb/article-9066005/scaffold

Johnsen, S. K., & Goree, K. (2005). *Independent study for gifted learners.* Waco, TX: Prufrock Press.

Kitano, M., & Kirby, D. F. (1986). *Gifted education: A comprehensive view.* Boston: Little, Brown.

Paul, R. (1997). *Critical thinking: What every person needs to survive in a rapidly changing world.* Sonoma, CA: Center for Critical Thinking.

Renzulli, J. S. (1977). *The enrichment triad model: A guide for developing defensible programs for the gifted and talented.* Mansfield Center, CT: Creative Learning Press.

Renzulli, J. S., & Reis, S. M. (1991). The schoolwide enrichment model: A comprehensive plan for the development of creative productivity. In N. Colangelo & G. A. Davis (Eds.), *Handbook of gifted education* (pp. 111–141). Needham Heights, MA: Allyn & Bacon.

Rogers, K. B. (2002). *Re-forming gifted education: How parents and teachers can match the program to the child.* Scottsdale, AZ: Great Potential Press.

Stewart, E. D. (1981). Learning styles among gifted/talented students: Instructional technique preferences. *Exceptional Children, 48,* 134–138.

Winebrenner, S. (2001). *Teaching gifted kids in the regular classroom.* Minneapolis, MN: Free Spirit.

About the Authors

Susan K. Johnsen, Ph.D., is a professor in the Department of Educational Psychology at Baylor University. She directs the Ph.D. program and programs related to gifted and talented education. She has written more than 100 articles, monographs, technical reports, and books related to gifted education. She is the editor of *Identifying Gifted Students: A Practical Guide* and three tests that are used in identifying gifted students: Test of Mathematical Abilities for Gifted Students (TOMAGS), Test of Nonverbal Intelligence (TONI-3), and Screening Assessment for Gifted Students (SAGES-2). She is a frequent presenter at international, national, and state conferences. She is editor of *Gifted Child Today* and serves on the editorial boards of *Gifted Child Quarterly*, *Journal for the Education of the Gifted*, and *Roeper Review* and on the Board of Examiners of the National Council for Accreditation of Teacher Education. She is president-elect of The Association for the Gifted (Council for Exceptional Children) and is past-president of the Texas Association for Gifted and Talented.

Kathryn Lee Johnson, Ed.S., is an adjunct professor in the School of Education at the University of Rhode Island. She teaches the Language Arts Methods and the Teaching of Literacy courses to preservice teachers and supervises student teachers in elementary classrooms. Other publications at Prufrock Press include *Writing Like Writers: Guiding Elementary Children Through a Writer's Workshop*, and *Writing With Authors Kids Love*. She has presented numerous workshops for teachers at state and national conferences, as well as consulting in school districts on the writing process.

With a lifelong love of words and books, Kay merges these two passions with calligraphy and bookbinding as she creates original, one-of-a-kind books. She's been dancing with the pen ever since she picked up that first chiseled nib more than 20 years ago. Her art has been exhibited in New England. A transplant from Kentucky, she now lives in bucolic southern Rhode Island with her husband and two teenage sons.

CPSIA information can be obtained
at www.ICGtesting.com
Printed in the USA
FFOW04n1851280317
33820FF